COUNTRY COMFORT

COUNTRY COMFORT

Hearty, wholesome meals in minutes

HARI BEAVIS

Carnival

Introduction

This book has been a dream in the making. Even before I was creating food content, my mum would find little recipe books of mine that I had been writing since I was a little girl. I always wanted to inspire people to be in their kitchen, surrounded by loved ones and making food that makes others happy or to indulge in a little self-care in the form of food.

Throughout my career I have been faced with people saying that there is a right and wrong way to cook, but I don't agree – there is no wrong way to cook. For me, it's a creative art where you combine your favourite flavours to make comforting dishes that brings happiness to those around you: whether it's for a friend that needs a little pick-me-up, a family member who has just hit a milestone and you're wanting to celebrate, or you have just had a long day and want to whip something up that nourishes your body while hitting all of those comforting elements we all crave from time to time. Food is for enjoying. Thus, *Country Comfort* was born.

The recipes in this book have been perfected thanks to generations of love and warmth from my friends and family: from rainy British days with the family coming in all muddy and tending to the animals, then whipping off the wellies and scrambling to get in the shower before the hot water runs out. After some friendly bickering we'd be sitting on the kitchen surfaces together, peeling vegetables for a family roast dinner, playlist on and a glass of something in our hands. This book grasps that sense of warmth and love and puts it into 90 recipes that are perfect for any occasion. The recipes are spread across five chapters, organized by the time it takes to make them.

COMFORT IN 10 is a collection of quick dishes suitable for those days when you don't have enough time or are too tired to cook.

COMFORT IN 20 is full of comfort food that make perfect weeknight dinners, including plenty of traybakes and one pan dishes.

COMFORT IN 30: when you have a little more time, and want to make something a bit more special, this is the chapter to go to.

COMFORT IN 40: these recipes that are slightly more complicated or may require a longer cooking time. They make ideal weekend meals and are perfect for feeding family and friends.

I've also included a chapter, 'Baking Everything Better', which showcases the best of my cakes and bakes.

Whilst the recipes in the book are all quick and easy to make, I've noted any elements that can be prepared in advance in grey at the end of each introduction.

Throughout the book you'll notice that many of my recipes feature chicken or salmon. These are my favourite sources of protein and so I often use them in my cooking. For those of you who prefer other flavourings, I have included an Alternative Ingredients panel with suggestions for vegetarian substitutions and other items that can be easily be swapped into the dishes if you don't have everything to hand.

Going back to basics with quick, simple recipes that don't feel rushed or thoughtless, food has the ability to take you back to a time where you felt loved, warm and safe. It doesn't need to be roasts on a rainy British day, it might be something that reminds you of a favourite holiday, or being around the Christmas table, or something your nana used to whip up when you were young. Food brings back memories, so let's get together and make comfort food that makes us feel happy, whether you're dressing up and making a feast for friends, or simply just out of the shower in your PJs, whipping up a family favourite. There is something wholesome and simply delicious in this book for everyone.

COMFORT

in 10

THE FLUFFY
BUTT
HUT

Raspberry, Nectarine & Mozzarella Salad

Bring friends and family together by throwing a few simple and delicate ingredients into a bowl: this is the perfect summer family barbecue salad. You can have this as a main course or a side. The tartness of the raspberries mixed with the creaminess of the mozzarella just tastes remarkable, yet it's so simple and can be made in under 10 minutes!

200g (7oz) raspberries
1 fresh orange
2–3 tbsp extra virgin olive oil
1 tsp balsamic vinegar
60–70g (2¼–2½oz) rocket (arugula) leaves
4 nectarines, stoned and sliced into 5mm (¼in) pieces
10–15g (⅓–½oz) fresh basil, roughly chopped
1 ball of buffalo mozzarella
salt and pepper

EQUIPMENT
chopping board—knife—1 small bowl
a blunt utensil - a pestle or the end of a rolling pin (or the back of a spoon or fork)—1 large bowl

MAKE THE DRESSING
Put the raspberries in the small bowl and crush them into a purée with a blunt utensil such as a pestle. Add the juice from the orange, the olive oil, balsamic vinegar, and season with salt and pepper. Give it a really good mix and that's your dressing done.

ASSEMBLE THE SALAD
Put the rocket, nectarines and basil in a large bowl and tear in your mozzarella. Pour the dressing over the salad and give it a really good toss together until coated, serve and enjoy.

ALTERNATIVE INGREDIENTS
Fresh orange: use shop-bought orange juice. It doesn't have to be fresh, but it does taste a little better if it is. Other citrus fruit, such as limes, also work well here.
Extra virgin olive oil: use normal olive oil
Balsamic vinegar: use white or red wine vinegar. Or leave out and replace its tartness with 30g more raspberries.
Rocket: use a mixed leaf salad or a romaine lettuce
Fresh basil: use mint

My Loved Ones' Carbonara

My sister and I used to ask our mum for carbonara every day. The creamy spaghetti with salty bacon would comfort us and fill our bellies, and we'd have a great night's sleep. My partner, Jake, started to make it for me when I had had a long day and didn't want to turn the oven on. It's always been made for me by loved ones, and even if they scrambled the egg (it's happened) I will still eat the bowlful. There is something about a dish made with love that just hits the spot. This version combines my mum's recipe, my sister's recipe and Jake's recipes to make the ultimate Loved Ones' Carbonara.

3 egg yolks
45g (1½oz) parmesan cheese, grated, plus
    extra to serve
230g (8oz) bucatini pasta
300g (10½oz) unsmoked pancetta, diced
1–2 garlic cloves, peeled and finely
    chopped
truffle oil, for drizzling
crushed black pepper
salt

EQUIPMENT
grater—chopping board—knife—bowl
fork—saucepan—frying pan—spoon

GET THE EGG MIX READY AND COOK THE PASTA
Mix the egg yolks and parmesan in a bowl with a twist of black pepper and set aside. Bring a saucepan of salted water to the boil and add the pasta.

FRY THE PANCETTA THEN ADD THE PASTA AND EGG MIX
Fry the pancetta in the frying pan over a medium-high heat until crispy, then reduce the heat to medium-low and throw in the garlic (if the garlic starts to burn the pan is too hot). Reduce the heat again to low and, when the pasta is al dente, spoon it into the pancetta (setting the pasta water aside) and garlic and mix it around over a low heat. Gradually add the eggs so that the sauce thickens and doesn't scramble (do it little by little if you're worried it might). Add a splash of pasta water and keep mixing the pasta until the sauce is thick and glossy, and coating all of the pasta.

SERVE
Serve the carbonara in a pasta bowl with a generous drizzle of truffle oil and extra grated parmesan on top, finishing with a good crack of black pepper.

Chicken Quesadillas

Quesadillas are one of the most versatile meals, and are a wonderfully quick way to show a loved one you've thought of them: maybe they've had a bad day and want to come home to something warm and cheesy that feels like a hug for their stomach or maybe the kids have had an after-school club in the cold and need a snack before dinner. Add anything you have in the fridge to the middle of two wraps (it's these quick, easy recipes where you can practice your cooking skills, through using things you like or that need eating up). If you use shredded cooked chicken, it only takes 10 minutes but puts smiles on faces for hours.

50g (1¾oz) butter
6 garlic cloves, peeled and finely chopped
1 onion, peeled and chopped
4 skinless chicken breasts, very finely sliced (or use shredded cooked chicken)
1 green (bell) pepper, deseeded and diced
1 tsp ground cumin
1 tsp garlic granules
½ tsp salt
½ tsp freshly ground black pepper
12 wraps
200g (7oz) mature (sharp) Cheddar cheese, grated
100g (3½oz) grated mozzarella
1 tbsp sliced jalapeños from a jar (if you like a kick)

EQUIPMENT
chopping board—knife—grater
frying pan

COOK THE CHICKEN
Melt a little of the butter in a frying pan over a medium heat, add the garlic and onion and cook for 5 minutes until soft, then add the chicken and pepper and cook for 1–2 minutes until the pepper is soft and the chicken is cooked through. Add the cumin, garlic granules, salt and pepper and mix together for a few more minutes.

ASSEMBLE AND COOK THE QUESADILLAS
Spread some butter on one side of a wrap and pop it butter-side down in the frying pan over a medium heat, add the chicken and pepper filling and sprinkle over some grated Cheddar and mozzarella along with some chopped jalapeños. Spread butter on another wrap and pop this one on top of the filling with the butter-side facing up. When the base is golden and crispy and that cheese is beginning to melt, flip it over so the other buttered wrap is facing down. When the cheese is melted and the wraps are toasted, remove from the pan. Repeat with the remaining wraps and filling, slice into triangles and enjoy this easy and delicious quesadilla.

ALTERNATIVE INGREDIENTS
Butter: use mayonnaise
Chicken: use beef steak or mince and just adjust seasoning and cooking times accordingly
Green (bell) pepper: use any colour pepper and any other veggies. Other things I like to add are spring onion (scallion), bok choy, mushrooms and tomatoes (the list is endless).
Seasoning: use your favourite flavours. I add a little paprika or ground coriander (cilantro) from time to time.
Cheese: use your favourite cheese, I once added blue cheese and it was delicious!

Breakfast Beans & Eggs

This ten-minute recipe is a great breakfast or brunch dish when you want to impress your other half, or just want to treat yourself because it's a Sunday – and why not? You've had toast and cereal all week and fancy something a bit tastier that has a whole load more nutrients!

1 x 400g (14oz) tin baked beans
200g (7oz) tinned chopped tomatoes
30g (1oz) mature (sharp) Cheddar cheese, grated
1 tsp Worcestershire sauce
knob of butter
large pinch each of salt and pepper
2 medium eggs
crispy sourdough and lots of butter, to serve

EQUIPMENT
grater—ovenproof serving bowl or dish
spoon

PREHEAT THE OVEN AND BAKE THE BASE MIXTURE
Preheat the oven to 200°C (180°C fan/400°F/gas mark 6). Put the baked beans, chopped tomatoes, Cheddar cheese, Worcestershire sauce, butter and salt and pepper in the ovenproof bowl or dish. Mix really well and whack in the oven for 5–6 minutes until everything is warmed through and you can see that cheese starting to melt.

LET'S GET EGGY
Stir to make sure the butter and cheese is evenly dispersed and then use the back of the spoon to make two little dents in the mixture. Break an egg into each dent and return the dish to the oven for 3 minutes or so (until the eggs are cooked to your liking).

SERVE
Remove from the oven and serve immediately, with lots of buttered sourdough for dunking. Such a warming breakfast that's comforting and sets you up for a Sunday on the sofa when it's grey and miserable outside!

ALTERNATIVE INGREDIENTS
Baked beans: use any tinned beans – black beans and butterbeans work really well
Cheddar cheese: use any cheese you fancy, such as mozzarella or feta

Honey-kissed
Baked Camembert

If it's for a special occasion, or I've just got friends coming over, a baked Brie or Camembert is always, always going to be on the table! I whack it in the oven for less than ten minutes then have a beautifully indulgent melted cheese for dunking French bread or garlic bread into. I have included other topping ideas so you can play around with the flavours and toppings so it feels like a different starter, dinner or sharing snack every time!

1 x 250g (9oz) Camembert
3 garlic cloves, halved
1 tbsp runny honey
pinch of salt
leaves from 1 rosemary sprig
French bread or garlic bread, warmed, to
　serve

EQUIPMENT
cheese baking dish with a lid – these dishes make great Christmas presents!
sharp knife

PREHEAT THE OVEN AND PREP THE CAMEMBERT
Preheat the oven to 220°C (200°C fan/425°F/gas mark 7). Remove all the Camembert packaging and place it in the cheese baking dish. Cut lines 5mm (¼ inch) deep and 2.5cm (1 inch) apart in the cheese then cut lines across these lines (so you have diamond-shaped cuts). Shove a little halved garlic clove into some of the crosses, drizzle the honey over the top and sprinkle with the salt and rosemary leaves.

BAKE AND SERVE
Cover with the lid and bake for 6–8 minutes until melted. Remove from the oven and serve with lovely warm French bread or a garlic bread with lots of butter!

ALTERNATIVE INGREDIENTS
Pine nut and pesto: 1 tbsp shop-bought pesto, a handful of toasted pine nuts, sprinkle of basil leaves, 1 tbsp olive oil, pinch of salt
Alcoholic cranberries: leaves from a sprig of thyme, a handful of dried cranberries, 1 tbsp Cointreau, 1 tbsp honey, pinch of salt

Harissa Chickpea & Halloumi Salad

There is something amazing about letting a pan do all the work and sitting back just ten minutes later to enjoy a delightful, nourishing dinner. This quick colourful salad with halloumi and spicy chickpeas is filled with goodness, simply delicious, and is a great one to make ahead. If you keep spices like harissa, tamarind paste, or teriyaki in the fridge, it is so easy to whip up a meal that is instantly injected with flavour!

400g (14oz) tin chickpeas
    (garbanzo beans), drained and rinsed
1 tbsp harissa paste
pinch each of salt and pepper
1 tsp garlic granules
200g (7oz) halloumi,
    cut into 2cm (¾in) dice
1 tsp honey
pinch of dried chilli flakes
2 heads of romaine (cos) lettuce,
    roughly chopped
40g (1½oz) cucumber, cubed
4 spring onions (scallions), trimmed
    and finely chopped
40g (1½oz) cherry tomatoes, halved
40g (1½oz) pomegranate seeds

FOR THE DRESSING
1 tbsp hummus
1 tbsp lemon juice
1 tbsp olive oil
pinch each of salt and pepper

EQUIPMENT
chopping board—knife—frying pan
bowl—wooden spoon or tongs
salad bowl

COOK THE CHICKPEAS AND HALLOUMI
Heat the frying pan over a medium-high heat. Mix the chickpeas, harissa paste, salt, pepper and garlic granules in a bowl, then throw them into the frying pan. Move them on one side of the pan and add the halloumi to the other side. Drizzle the halloumi with the honey and sprinkle with the chilli flakes. Try and keep the two components separate and cook for about 8 minutes until they're both slightly golden.

MAKE THE DRESSING
While the chickpeas and harissa are cooking, put the hummus, lemon juice, olive oil, salt and pepper in the salad bowl and mix (add a little more oil and lemon if you want it to be runnier).

TOSS EVERYTHING TOGETHER AND SERVE
Throw the romaine lettuce, cucumber, spring onion and cherry tomatoes into the bowl, tossing them through the dressing, then throw in the chickpeas, halloumi and pomegranate seeds. Mix until everything is coated in the dressing. Serve.

The salad will keep in the fridge in an airtight container for up to 3 days.

ALTERNATIVE INGREDIENTS
Chickpeas (garbanzo beans): use the same weight of cooked bulgur wheat or edamame beans (there's no need to add these to the frying pan, just mix them into the salad), or add black beans to the pan
Harissa paste: use sriracha sauce, Tabasco or a Korean gochujang
Romaine (cos) lettuce: use any salad ingredients – rocket (arugula) or baby gem are my favourites
Cucumber, spring onion (scallion), tomatoes: use any vegetables, such as shredded carrot or cabbage to give the salad an additional crunch.
Halloumi: use a vegan cheese or sweet potato or butternut squash – these soak up the honey, harissa and spices and work so well with the chickpeas, although they do need to be cooked for longer

Showstopper
Summer Salad

It really doesn't matter if you're a beginner cook for this dish because, guess what, there is no cooking. It's something I came across in Italy. With its beautiful concentric circles of white, red and green it really is the perfect showstopper summer salad for any barbecue or garden party. Everyone will be impressed and it's just refreshingly delicious!

5 tbsp extra virgin olive oil
juice of 1 lime
6 large 'buffalo steak' tomatoes
2 balls of mozzarella
3 ripe avocados, stoned and peeled
salt and pepper
a handful of fresh basil, to serve

EQUIPMENT
small bowl (for the dressing)—chopping board—knife —serving plate

MAKE THE DRESSING
Put the olive oil and lime juice in a small bowl, season with salt and pepper, mix and set aside.

SLICE THE SALAD INGREDIENTS
Slice the tomatoes, mozzarella and avocado into evenly thick slices. You want them to all be the same size. Dunk each slice of tomato and avocado into the dressing you prepared (the dressing will help prevent the avocado from going brown).

PLATE UP
Starting on the outside of your serving plate, place a slice of tomato, a slice of avocado then a slice of mozzarella, overlapping them around the outside of the dish. Repeat until you have a full circle then create another a little closer to the centre. Finally, fill the middle with a slice of tomato, mozzarella and the last few pieces of avocado. If you have any leftover dressing, drizzle it on top of the salad and place basil leaves on top. It really is so simple.

Chickpea &
Spinach Curry

SERVES 2

I made this a lot when I lived in Oxford. It's super speedy and cheap to whip up and was a great meal when I didn't have a lot in the fridge – most of the ingredients are cupboard staples. The quantities below make two portions but by all means increase the quantities and stash a few portions in the freezer. Throw over some rice and you have a bowl of goodness flavoured with herbs and spices to make you feel all warm and cosy inside.

drizzle of olive oil
1 white onion, peeled and finely diced
6 garlic cloves, peeled and finely chopped
2.5cm (1in) piece of fresh red chilli, finely chopped, plus extra slices to garnish
2.5cm (1in) piece of ginger, finely chopped
1 tsp ground cumin
1 tsp ground coriander
1 tsp paprika
1 tsp salt
pinch of dried chilli flakes
1 tbsp tomato purée (paste)
400g (14oz) tin chickpeas (garbanzo beans)
400g (14oz) tin chopped tomatoes
400g (14oz) tin coconut milk
100g (3½oz) fresh spinach
rice, to serve
1 lime, halved, to serve

EQUIPMENT
chopping board—knife—deep frying pan
spoon

MAKE THE CURRY
Heat the oil in the deep frying pan over a medium heat, add the onion, garlic, chilli and ginger and cook for 5 minutes until softened, then throw in the cumin, coriander, paprika, salt and chilli flakes. Stir, then add the tomato purée and the chickpeas, tomatoes and coconut milk. Mix until you have a nice sauce then throw in your spinach. Cook for 5 minutes, until the spinach has wilted and the sauce has thickened to your liking.

SERVE
Serve with fluffy rice and lime halves to squeeze over.

The curry will keep in the fridge in an airtight container for up to 2–3 days.

ALTERNATIVE INGREDIENTS
Olive oil: use ghee, butter, coconut oil, garlic oil or chilli oil
Fresh chilli and ginger - adding these to a curry elevates the dish, but if you don't want to add them you don't have to, I always throw them in because I keep them in the house!
Onion: use any kind of onion or shallots
Spices: use a curry powder
Coconut milk: use coconut cream
Spinach: use a few cubes of frozen spinach

Creamy
Tuna Pasta

You'll probably be familiar with tuna pasta bake and know how easy it is to make, but this ten-minute dinner is even quicker and easier. It doesn't need any baking, although if you want a cheesy top by all means whack it in a hot oven for an extra 10 minutes with a load of cheese on top. Part of the beauty of the recipes in this book is that you can make them your own, they're versatile and always looking to be made into something that YOU and your family love. Here, I like to use a pasta that has grooves or holes in it so the gorgeous sauce sticks to that pasta!

200g (7oz) dried pasta
1–2 tbsp olive oil
4–5 garlic cloves, peeled and finely
    chopped
250g (9oz) plum or cherry tomatoes
2 tbsp tomato purée (paste)
250ml (8fl oz/1 cup) double (heavy) cream
2 x 145g (5¼oz) tins tuna
a handful of basil leaves, chopped
salt

EQUIPMENT
chopping board—knife—saucepan—frying
pan—wooden spoon

COOK THE PASTA
Cook the pasta in very well-seasoned boiling water and while it's cooking make the sauce. By the time the pasta is done the sauce will be too.

MAKE THE SAUCE
Heat the olive oil in a frying pan over a medium-low heat, add the garlic and tomatoes and cook for 3–5 minutes until the tomatoes are softened and their juices are making a sauce with the garlic and oil. Add the tomato purée to get a silky tomato sauce, then add the double cream and mix until combined. When you have a lovely creamy, tomatoey sauce, add the tuna and mix it through until all those chunks have broken up.

COMBINE THE PASTA AND SAUCE, AND SERVE
Drain the pasta and then add it to the sauce. Stir to coat, and finish with a sprinkling of basil leaves. It keeps well so you can have it for lunch the next day.

ALTERNATIVE INGREDIENTS
Tomatoes: if you're not a tomato lover or can't eat tomatoes (my Nana can't), a great alternative is olives – they have a similarly delicate flavour and soft texture
Double (heavy) cream: use crème fraîche, cream cheese or single (light) cream if all the double cream is sold out! Anything with a creamy consistency will work perfectly.
Tuna: use tinned salmon, or if you have time cook another protein, or use leftover chicken from the Sunday roast!
Basil: use any of your favourite herbs – parsley would work well here

Quickie Prawny Spaghetti

SERVES 2

Mum made this for us as kids. It's so simple, can be whipped up in 10 minutes and is great for all the family. My sister and I were like chalk and cheese with our taste buds: she liked simple foods (margarita pizza, pasta and cheese, beans on toast) while I was eating everything and anything (olives, spicy curries and flavours that were probably above my age bracket) – this satisfied us both. No complex flavours, just a handful of ingredients that kept us happy!

200g (7oz) dried spaghetti
20g (¾oz) butter
5 garlic cloves, peeled and finely chopped
1 chilli, finely diced (deseed for less heat)
200g (7oz) raw king prawns (shrimp), peeled and deveined
200ml (7fl oz/generous ¾ cup) double (heavy) cream
60g (2¼oz) parmesan cheese, grated

EQUIPMENT
saucepan—chopping board—knife
frying pan—wooden spoon—grater

COOK THE SPAGHETTI
Bring a saucepan of salted water to the boil (I add a drizzle of olive oil too), then add the spaghetti and cook according to the packet instructions.

MAKING THE SAUCE
While the spaghetti cooks, melt the butter in a frying pan over a medium heat, then add the garlic and chilli and let them soften for a couple of minutes before adding the prawns. Add the cream and parmesan and mix until the parmesan is all melted. Your prawns will cook gently in this sauce.

COMBINE THE SPAGHETTI AND PRAWNS AND SERVE
Transfer the spaghetti to the sauce (don't worry if some of the pasta water comes along with it – the starchy, salty water will just add thickness and creaminess), mix it through, serve up and enjoy. I love to sprinkle over a pinch of paprika or some fresh chopped parsley!

ALTERNATIVE INGREDIENTS
Butter: use olive oil
King prawns (shrimp): use any type of protein, perhaps a bag of frozen seafood including scallops, calamari and mussels to expand the flavours!
Double (heavy) cream: use single (light) cream, crème fraîche or cream cheese

'Can't be Bothered to Cook' Chilli Noodles

I don't know where I would be without these comforting noodles. On evenings when I'm starving and I really can't be bothered to cook, I whip these up. They take ten minutes (if that), they're spicy, they clear the sinuses, and above all are made with sauce that is packed with flavour, making sure I feel satisfied and like I have had a proper meal.

120g (4¼oz) dried wheat noodles
1 tbsp toasted sesame oil
1 tsp finely chopped fresh ginger
4 garlic cloves, peeled and finely chopped
1 tbsp smooth peanut butter
½ tsp finely chopped fresh chilli (or substitute the olive oil for chilli oil)
¼ tsp ground turmeric
1 tbsp dark soy sauce
½ tsp light brown sugar

TO SERVE
1 tbsp lime juice
1 tsp finely chopped fresh coriander (cilantro)
1 spring onion (scallion), trimmed and finely chopped
1 tsp white sesame seeds

EQUIPMENT
chopping board—knife—saucepan
frying pan

COOK THE NOODLES
Cook the noodles according to the packet instructions. Drain.

MAKE THE SAUCE
Put the frying pan over a medium heat and add the sesame oil, ginger, garlic, peanut butter, chilli, turmeric, soy sauce and brown sugar. Mix until the sugar has dissolved, throw in the cooked, drained noodles and stir to coat them in the sauce. If it's a little thick, add a little bit of water, if it's too watery just keep cooking until you get the sauce to the consistency that you like.

SERVE
Pop the noodles in a bowl and finish with the lime juice, chopped coriander, spring onions and sesame seeds!

The noodles will keep in the fridge for 2–3 days.

ALTERNATIVE INGREDIENTS
Noodles: use your favourite noodles – try udon, egg, rice or even Singapore
Sesame oil: use chilli oil or garlic oil
Peanut butter - this can be taken out all together if you're not a fan!
Dark soy sauce: use light soy sauce
Garnish: use whatever you fancy, such as crispy onions, peanuts or cashews

A British Pan con Tomate

I call this my 'British Pan Con Tomate' because there is no way I can go up against the beautiful Mediterranean equivalents. It involves a lot of the same elements and is divine in the summer when tomatoes are juicy and ripe. It's a really simple dish that feels equally comforting and fresh. If you like bruschetta, you're sure to like this. Here, though, the 'faff' of lots of chopping needed to make a bruschetta is taken out but you've got the same key ingredients – good-quality bread, tomato, olive oil and a hint of garlic. This makes such a lovely lunch, snack or starter!

1 x 250–300g (9–10½oz) loaf of ciabatta, halved and each half quartered
4 tbsp good-quality olive oil
2 garlic cloves, halved
2–3 large good-quality tomatoes (about 400g/14oz)
pinch of salt

EQUIPMENT
grill (broiler)—grater—bowl—knife

TOAST THE CIABATTA
Drizzle 2 tablespoons of olive oil over your bread quarters and toast them under a hot grill until golden brown and crispy. Remove from the grill and rub a garlic clove over each piece while they're still warm. Set aside.

ADD THE TOMATOES AND SERVE
Cut the top off each tomato so you don't have stalk in the mixture, then grate the tomatoes on the large grating hole into a bowl, adding the remaining olive oil and salt. Spoon the mixture on top of the toasted ciabatta and serve!

ALTERNATIVE INGREDIENTS
Ciabatta: use thick slices of sourdough

Mediterranean Pasta Salad

This is such a wonderfully fresh salad to make in the summer, whether you prep it for lunches or serve it as a side dish for a family barbecue. It takes ten minutes to whip up, it's bright and colourful, and adding pasta just gives you that comforting full-belly feeling.

Make the salad up to 24 hours in advance and chill in the fridge – if you're going to a barbecue you can make it in the morning and it will still be perfect by dinnertime.

200g (7oz) dried fusilli pasta
250g (9oz) cucumber, finely chopped
250g (9oz) cherry tomatoes, finely chopped
a large handful of spinach, finely chopped
1 red onion, peeled and finely diced (or a bunch of spring onions/scallions for a milder taste)
200g (7oz) feta, crumbled
250g (9oz) kalamata olives, halved and stoned (optional)

FOR THE DRESSING
75ml (2½fl oz/⅓ cup) olive oil
3 tbsp lime juice
½ tsp dried oregano
1 garlic clove, peeled and grated
large pinch of salt
large pinch of crushed black pepper

EQUIPMENT
chopping board—knife—grater—salad bowl—hand whisk or spoon—salad tongs or 2 spoons

COOK THE PASTA
Bring a saucepan of salted water to the boil (I add a drizzle of olive oil too), then add the pasta and cook according to the packet instructions. Drain and set aside.

MAKE THE DRESSING
Pop all the dressing ingredients in the salad bowl and mix well.

COMBINE THE SALAD INGREDIENTS AND SERVE
Throw all the salad ingredients (other than the pasta) into the salad bowl, add the cooked pasta, and toss them through the dressing. It's as simple as that!

The leftover salad will keep in the fridge for up to 2 days.

ALTERNATIVE INGREDIENTS
Spinach: use chopped (bell) pepper, grated carrots or sweetcorn

Welsh Rarebit - our Rugby Game Day Staple!

SERVES 1-2

When the Six Nations come round, our family gets a bit competitive. I am half Welsh, half English, so it gets complicated when we sit down to watch England vs Wales! To defuse the situation, I bring out my cheesy Welsh rarebit. For those that don't know what a rarebit is, it's glorified cheese on toast, and it is marvellous. I used to make it as a starter with little pieces of ciabatta during ski season and everyone would go nuts for it!

Whip up 'the rarebit' mix an hour or two in advance if you want to prep before a sports game, then at half time just whack it in the oven and enjoy piping hot!

1 thick slice of sourdough bread
1 tbsp olive oil
1 large egg
30g (1oz) mature (sharp) Cheddar
  cheese, grated
½ tsp (or a shake) of Worcestershire sauce
1 tsp wholegrain mustard
salt
pinch of chopped chives, to serve

EQUIPMENT
chopping board—knife—grill (broiler)
medium bowl—whisk or spoon—grater

GRILL THE SOURDOUGH
Drizzle the sourdough with the olive oil and sprinkle with salt, then place on a baking tray under a hot grill until golden brown and crispy – it needs to be crispy enough so it doesn't go soggy when you add the egg mix.

MAKE THE RAREBIT AND SERVE
Mix the egg, half the grated cheese, and the Worcestershire sauce and mustard in the bowl. Spoon the mixture onto the grilled sourdough, spreading it out into an even layer. Sprinkle over the remaining cheese and put it back under the grill until the egg mixture is no longer running and the cheese on top is bubbling. Remove from the grill and add another sprinkle of salt and a showering of chopped chives. Serve hot and enjoy straight away!

ALTERNATIVE INGREDIENTS
Sourdough: use whatever bread you fancy, as long as it's quite thick – ciabatta works well
Cheddar cheese: use Gouda, a Swiss hard cheese, Gloucestershire or even a feta.
Wholegrain mustard: use Dijon, or ½ teaspoon of English mustard.

Peter Pepper's
Pickled Pasta

This is such an undemanding recipe to whip up on a cold, wintery evening. It's warming too – with a hint of heat flickering through – and can be made in one pan. I could never master the Peter Piper tongue-twister nursery rhyme as a child, but this Peter Pepper's Pickled Pasta is much easier… and it adds a bit of fun to dinnertime!

10 dried lasagne sheets (we often have some of these in the back of the cupboard)
drizzle of olive oil
1 bulb of garlic, cloves peeled and finely chopped
1 red chilli, deseeded and finely chopped
4 jarred roasted (bell) peppers, finely diced
1 tsp red wine vinegar
400ml (14fl oz/1¾ cups) tomato passata (puréed tomatoes)
50g (1¾oz) parmesan cheese, grated
large handful fresh basil, chopped, plus extra to serve
1–2 tsp balsamic vinegar glaze (to taste)

EQUIPMENT
chopping board—knife—grater—saucepan frying pan—wooden spoon

TIME FOR THE PASTA
Break the lasagne sheets into different sizes, lengths and shapes and throw them into a saucepan of boiling, salted water.

MAKE THE SAUCE
While the pasta's cooking, heat the olive oil in the frying pan over a medium heat, add the garlic, chilli, and diced peppers and cook for a minute or two, then add the red wine vinegar, passata and parmesan and most of the basil and simmer until the pasta is al dente then, using a slotted spoon, add your pasta to the sauce. Mix well to coat the pasta in the sauce.

SERVE
Serve the dish with a drizzle of balsamic glaze and a final sprinkle of basil to garnish.

ALTERNATIVE INGREDIENTS
Lasagne sheets: use any kind of pasta
Garlic bulb: use 1–2 teaspoons garlic puree or jarred garlic
Red chili: use ½–1 teaspoon dried chilli flakes
Red wine vinegar: use white wine vinegar
Basil: use dried basil or use fresh parsley
Jarred roasted (bell) peppers: use sun-dried tomatoes
Parmesan: use vegan parmesan or 1–2 tablespoons of nutritional yeast

My Chopped Cobb Salad

Summertime salads are a must in my house. When it gets hot I need cool, crunchy refreshing meals and a cobb salad is just that – this one's a barbecue-season staple. I love being able to chop everything up super small so I can eat it with a spoon. I've taken out the bits I don't enjoy about a classic cobb and swapped them for a few of my favourite ingredients: it's a great way to use up what's in the salad drawer while making it look like you've put time and effort into the dish. And you don't have to be a skilled cook to pull it off – the most complicated thing is chopping everything up! Leave out the meat for veggies.

2 heads romaine (cos) lettuce, finely chopped
2 cooked chicken breasts, finely chopped
6 rashers of crispy cooked streaky bacon, finely chopped
50g (1¾oz) feta, crumbled
1 ripe avocado, stoned, peeled and finely chopped
¼ red onion, peeled and finely diced
3 spring onions (scallions), trimmed and finely chopped
¼ cucumber, finely diced

FOR THE DRESSING
1 tsp white wine vinegar
1 tsp lemon juice
1 tsp garlic purée
1 ½ tbsp Dijon mustard
6 tbsp olive oil
large pinch of salt
large pinch of freshly ground black pepper

MAKE THE DRESSING
Make it in the bottom of the salad bowl (so you don't have to do any more washing up!). Put all the dressing ingredients in the bowl and whisk really well until slightly frothy.

ADD THE REST OF THE INGREDIENTS
Throw all the salad ingredients into the bowl, mix them through the dressing and that is it! The easiest salad ever.

ALTERNATIVE INGREDIENTS
Other ingredients you could use or swap out would be:
Tomatoes, (bell) peppers, radishes, olives, rocket (arugula), watermelon, sweetcorn, grilled halloumi

EQUIPMENT
chopping board—knife—large salad bowl
whisk—salad tongs (or two spoons)

Spring Asparagus
& Blue Cheese

As a little dish to accompany a protein main, or have with a barbecue, this asparagus dish is beautiful, particularly in the spring. Blue cheese most often makes an appearance around Christmas time, in the form of Stilton wheels or as a cheese for festive crackers, but asparagus is a great pairing. With just six ingredients, this dish takes less than ten minutes to make, and requires next to no effort!

250g (9oz) asparagus spears
knob of butter
1–2 garlic cloves, peeled and crushed
30g (1oz) blue cheese (Stilton or
    Roquefort)
30g (1oz) pine nuts
½ lemon

EQUIPMENT
frying pan—serving dish

COOK THE ASPARAGUS
Heat the frying pan over a medium-high heat and while it heats up, remove the woody ends of the asparagus spears by holding a spear with one hand and gently bending the cut end of the asparagus with the other hand until it snaps. Melt the butter in the pan with the crushed garlic, add the asparagus and toss in the pan for about 5 minutes until cooked – I like to slightly char the asparagus, while keeping its crunchy consistency.

PLATE UP
Put the asparagus on a serving dish, crumble over the blue cheese and allow it to soften on the asparagus while you toast the pine nuts in the pan over a medium heat until golden brown (be careful, as they burn really easily). Sprinkle the pine nuts over the warm asparagus and blue cheese and finish with a good squeeze of lemon juice over it all!

ALTERNATIVE INGREDIENTS
Asparagus: use Tenderstem broccoli
Blue cheese: use feta or another cheese with a similar texture

COMFORT

in 20

One-pan Salmon Curry

SERVES 4

This salmon curry is so versatile – just swap out a few bits and bobs (see 'Alternative Ingredients') to make it vegan or vegetarian – and it is also jam-packed with goodness, from herbs and spices to garlic, all of which help cure the common cold in our household. It's warming and packed with flavour, and the spices are great to have to hand in your cupboard for playing around with to make something new and flavourful each week: just follow the basic method and you'll be fine!

3 tbsp olive oil
2 large salmon fillets, cut into large, chunky cubes
2 red onions, peeled and finely diced
8 garlic cloves, peeled and finely chopped
1 tsp garam masala
1 tsp ground cumin
1 tsp ground turmeric
1 tsp ground coriander
½ tsp paprika
2.5cm (1in) piece of fresh ginger, finely minced
1 chilli, finely chopped
4–5 tbsp tomato purée (paste)
400ml (14fl oz) tin coconut milk
2 handfuls of fresh spinach (about 60g/2¼oz)
100g (3½oz) tomatoes
2 tbsp ground almonds (almond meal)
salt and pepper

EQUIPMENT
chopping board—knife—1 large saucepan
wooden spoon

SEAR THE SALMON
Heat the oil in the large saucepan over a medium-high heat, add the diced salmon and sear for a minute or two, then remove from the pan and set aside.

MAKE THE SAUCE
Add the onion and garlic to the pan and cook for a couple of minutes until soft, then throw in all the spices (including the ginger and chilli) and cook for couple of minutes longer. Stir in the tomato purée and coconut milk, then add the spinach and tomatoes and cook for a couple of minutes until the spinach is wilted.

FINISHING TOUCHES
Add the ground almonds and return the salmon to the pan, then cover with a lid and cook for 5 minutes. Serve with rice and sprinkle in fresh coriander.

The dish will keep in the fridge for up to 2–3 days or can be frozen for up to 3 months (defrost in the fridge and reheat until piping hot before serving).

ALTERNATIVE INGREDIENTS
Salmon: use chicken, cod, hake or halibut, or for a vegan/veggie swap use tofu, squash or sweet potato
Spinach: use a few cubes of frozen spinach
Ground almonds – if you're allergic to nuts or just don't like the idea don't feel like you need to add them in, they just add an element of sweetness (similar to a Korma)

Leftover Rainbow Pinwheels

My nana used to make these with cheese and onion when our church had a service. I remember being really young and squeezing around all the adults' legs to try and get to the snack table before they all got eaten. There is something so comforting about eating something wrapped in puff pastry. They make perfect little canapé starters or snacks (they keep in the fridge for up to 1 week) and this is another one of my recipes where the ingredients are interchangeable – add your favourite flavours and make it your own. I really enjoy adding bacon and jalapeños to give them some saltiness and a good kick.

80g (2¾oz) sliced ham, finely chopped
3 spring onions (scallions), trimmed and finely chopped
1 red (bell) pepper, deseeded and finely chopped
80g (2¾oz) spinach, finely chopped
1 x 320g (11¼oz) sheet of all-butter puff pastry
80g (2¾oz) Cheddar cheese, grated
80g (2¾oz) red Leicester cheese, grated
1 egg, beaten

EQUIPMENT
chopping board—knife—large bowl
baking tray—little ramekin or bowl
pastry brush

PREHEAT THE OVEN AND ASSEMBLE THE PINWHEELS
Preheat the oven to 200°C (180°C fan/400°F/gas mark 6). Throw the ham, spring onions, pepper and spinach into a large bowl.

Unroll the sheet of pastry and spread the contents of the bowl across the surface of the pastry, then sprinkle over the grated cheeses. Roll up your pastry so it's like one long sausage then slice into 12 little rounds (2-2.5cm/¾-1in) that are filled with rainbow veggies. Place the rounds on a baking tray, spaced out to allow the pastry to puff up.

BAKE THE PINWHEELS
Brush each pinwheel with beaten egg and cook in the oven for 8 minutes until puffed up and golden brown. Serve and enjoy!

Steak and Caramelised Onion Sandwich

Steak and caramelised onion sandwich always sounds like something I would go for if we have a lovely long walk to a pub and it's on the menu. It's just good pub food and eating this in a pub garden after a long walk with a glass of something in my hand never fails to put me in a good mood. So I wanted to perfect the steak sandwich at home, and that I have!

1 sirloin steak, at room temperature
3–4 tbsp olive oil
1 loaf of ciabatta bread
1 tbsp mayonnaise
1 tsp Dijon mustard
a handful of rocket (arugula)
salt and pepper

FOR THE CARAMELISED ONIONS
2 red onions, peeled and thinly sliced
1 knob of butter
1 tbsp light brown sugar
2 tbsp balsamic vinegar

EQUIPMENT
chopping board—knife—saucepan
griddle pan—tongs—small bowl

PREPARE THE STEAK
Rub the steak generously with a good quality olive oil and season with salt and pepper. Pop it to one side while you prep the onions.

MAKE THE CARAMELISED ONIONS
Put the sliced onions in a saucepan with a knob of butter, the sugar, a pinch of salt and the balsamic vinegar. Cook over a low heat for 10–20 minutes until the onions begin to soften and caramelise.

COOK THE STEAK
Get a griddle pan screaming hot (test this by putting the edge of the steak on the pan – if it starts sizzling it's ready). When it's hot enough, pop the steak in and cook it how you like your steak cooked (I like to cook mine 2 minutes on each side, then sear the fat - use tongs to handle the steak so you don't hurt yourself). Remove from the pan and allow the steak to rest for as long as you cooked it for, while you prepare the rest of the sandwich.

FINISHING TOUCHES
Cut the ciabatta in half and drizzle it with the rest of the olive oil, then pop it in a warm oven (olive oil side facing up) to crisp, or pop it in the griddle pan for a minute or two (to soak up all those flavours from the steak).

While the bread is crisping up, mix the mayo and mustard together in a little bowl and slice your steak into 2cm (¾in) pieces. Once your bread has crisped up, you are ready to assemble. Spread the mustard mayo on the ciabatta, then layer on the caramelised onions, then the steak and – finally – a handful of rocket to finish.

ALTERNATIVE INGREDIENTS
While you can't really have an alternative ingredient for steak in a steak sandwich you can change the other ingredients that you pop in a ciabatta. For example:
Blue cheese—Tomato relish—Brie—Jalapeños—Watercress—Add chillies to the onions—Sharp Cheddar cheese—English mustard

Gnocchi Bake

Mouthfuls of soft dumplings mixed with your favourite Italian flavours? Yes, please! I'm not sure there is anything more comforting than a large spoonful of gnocchi coated in a tomato and basil sauce, brought together by stringy mozzarella and delicious salty ham.

a glug of olive oil
1 white onion, peeled and finely diced
6 garlic cloves, peeled and finely chopped
2 tbsp tomato puree (paste)
2 x 400g (14oz) tins chopped tomatoes
150g (5½oz) ham or gammon, cut into 2cm
   (¾in) pieces
1 tsp salt, plus extra to serve
1 tsp freshly ground black pepper
a handful of fresh basil, roughly chopped
400g (14oz) fresh potato gnocchi
125 g (4¼oz) ball of mozzarella

EQUIPMENT
chopping board—knife—deep frying pan
17 x 27cm (7 x 11in) ovenproof dish

PREHEAT THE OVEN AND MAKE THE SAUCE
Preheat the oven to 200°C (180°C fan/400°F/gas mark 6). Heat the oil in the deep frying pan over a medium-low heat, add the onion and garlic and cook for a few minutes until softened, then stir in the tomato puree. Throw in the chopped tomatoes and stir, then sprinkle in the ham, salt and pepper. Stir in three-quarters of the basil and all the gnocchi, then transfer to the ovenproof dish.

BAKE!
Thinly slice the mozzarella and lay it over the gnocchi, pop in the oven and bake for 10 minutes, until it starts to bubble, the gnocchi is cooked and the mozzarella is melted. Sprinkle with a pinch of salt and the remaining basil and serve!

ALTERNATIVE INGREDIENTS
Ham or gammon: use any sliced ham
Chopped tomatoes: use passata (puréed tomatoes) or a jar of tomato and basil pasta sauce
Mozzarella: use Cheddar cheese, parmesan or feta

Feta, Caramelised Onion
& Honey Tartlets

There is something about baked cheese and caramelised onion that just gets you ready for cosy nights in. Whether it's brie, Camembert or feta, something salty and creamy on a cosy carb works so well. These little tartlets can be made small for canapés, made into shapes for dinner parties, baked as a sheet of pastry for supper, or as little rectangles for a starter. Whatever the occasion, they fit the bill!

1 x 320g (11¼oz) sheet of all-butter puff pastry
4 tsp shop-bought caramelised onions
80g (2¾oz) feta
2 tsp runny honey
pinch of thyme leaves
1 egg, beaten, for egg wash
pinch of salt

EQUIPMENT
baking tray—knife—pastry brush

PREHEAT THE OVEN AND SCORE THE PASTRY
Preheat the oven to 180°C (160°C fan/350°F/gas mark 4) and unroll the pastry, keeping it on its parchment. Cut into four (this will be the four portions) and score a rectangle 2cm (¾in) from the edge of each portion with the blunt edge of your knife, making sure you don't cut through the pastry.

TOP THE PASTRY AND BAKE
Spread a teaspoon of caramelised onion in the middle of each scored portion and crumble over the feta. Drizzle honey over the top of each tart and throw on a few thyme leaves. Brush the edges of the pastry with egg wash and bake in the oven for 10–15 minutes, until the edges of the pastry tarts are puffed up and golden brown!

SERVE
Remove from the oven, sprinkle with salt and serve while warm. So yummy!

ALTERNATIVE INGREDIENTS
Caramelised onion: use a chutney
Feta: use any cheese you enjoy – I love a brie or Camembert
Thyme: use another fresh herb such as rosemary

Hug-in-a-bowl
Beef Stroganoff

I remember as a child going to a grown-up dinner party where there were mini bowls of beef stroganoff as a starter/canapé and everyone stood around eating this bowl of creamy goodness. I scoffed about three bowlfuls. I was too young to know or even think to ask what it was, but fast forward a decade and when I was served it again I realised I HAVE TO MAKE THIS! Make a large batch and keep it in the freezer for the winter months so when you have a busy week or just can't be bothered to cook, you can warm it up and have some comforting stroganoff ready in minutes (my partner and sister hate mushrooms and still gobble this up). Serve it with your favourite carb.

2–3 tbsp olive oil
6 garlic cloves, peeled and finely chopped
1 red onion, peeled and finely sliced
150g (5½oz) chestnut mushrooms, sliced
400g (14oz) diced beef
25g (1oz/2½ tbsp) plain (all-purpose) flour
knob of butter (optional)
250g (9oz) crème fraîche
1–2 tsp Worcestershire sauce
450ml (15fl oz/scant 2 cups) beef stock
    (bouillon) or 300ml/10fl oz/1¼ cups beef
    stock and 150ml/5fl oz/⅔ cup brandy
salt and pepper
rice and coriander (cilantro) or parsley,
    to serve

EQUIPMENT
chopping board—knife—frying pan
wooden spoon—bowl

COOK THE MUSHROOMS
Heat the oil in a frying pan over a medium heat, add the garlic and onion and let them soften for a couple of minutes. Once they're translucent, add the sliced mushrooms and cook for 5-7 minutes. You want them completely cooked before adding the beef.

COAT THE BEEF
While the mushrooms are cooking, toss the beef in a bowl with the flour and a pinch of salt until it's lightly and evenly coated.

SEAR THE BEEF AND ADD THE REMAINING INGREDIENTS
Remove the mushroom mixture from the pan and set aside. Add the floured beef to the pan and sear the beef pieces over a high heat for 3-4 minutes until they have started to brown (adding a knob of butter if the flour starts to catch) then return the mushroom mixture to the pan along with the crème fraîche, Worcestershire sauce and beef stock (and brandy, if using) and mix until it all comes together and you get a creamy sauce. Cook for 10 minutes, until the sauce starts to thicken and come together – it shouldn't take long.

SERVE
Remove from the heat and serve on a bed of rice. Garnish with your herb of choice and tuck right in.

ALTERNATIVE INGREDIENTS
Mushrooms: use artichoke hearts or lentils
Beef: use chicken or pork tenderloin (I have used leftover roast lamb here before and that was lovely too)
Crème fraîche: use double (heavy) or single (light) cream, or mascarpone

Baked Salmon with Garlic & Herb Crumb

SERVES 4

This is one of my absolute favourite dishes – a meaty piece of salmon with a crunchy breadcrumb top that is layered with garlic and parsley. Who doesn't love crunchy garlic bread and salmon? Well, whack them both together and wait for your taste buds to tingle. I love serving the salmon with buttery new potatoes or a whipped feta dip with salad. Divine!

4 skin-on salmon fillets (or one large enough to serve 4)
1 tbsp olive oil
salt and pepper

FOR THE CRUMB
1 large cooked garlic-bread ciabatta
4 garlic cloves (if you want it to be extra garlicky), peeled
a handful of parsley
½ tsp salt
½ tsp freshly ground black pepper
a drizzle of truffle oil (optional)

EQUIPMENT
baking tray—parchment—pastry brush
blender or food processor

PREHEAT THE OVEN AND COAT THE SALMON
Preheat the oven to 200°C (180°C fan/400°F/gas mark 6). Put the salmon fillets skin side down on the baking tray lined with parchment and brush them all over with olive oil and season with salt and pepper.

LET'S GET WHIZZZYYY
Put the ciabatta, garlic, parsley and salt and pepper in the blender and blitz to a rough crumb. Sprinkle the crumb mix on top of the salmon fillets, making a thick layer. You may need to press it down to ensure it sticks (if you're making this fancy, drizzle with truffle oil at this point).

SIT BACK AND LET THE OVEN DO THE WORK
Bake the salmon in the oven for 15 minutes until the top is golden brown and crispy. Serve and enjoy.

ALTERNATIVE INGREDIENTS
Salmon: use chicken or a white fish such as cod or halibut
Garlic bread: if you don't have a blender or food processor, have no fear – use 200–225g (7–8oz) good-quality breadcrumbs (you don't want them to be too fine) and combine with about 8 very finely chopped garlic cloves, finely chop the parsley and mix together in a bowl. Spoon this over your salmon.

My Kind of Chorizo & Egg Shakshuka

There are so many ways you can show someone you love them at breakfast. We're familiar with the usuals, such as pancakes, waffles and French toast, but if there is one thing that's guaranteed to get someone out of bed and down to the kitchen it's this twist on shakshuka.

1 tbsp olive oil
1 red onion, peeled and sliced
6 garlic cloves, peeled and finely chopped
1 red (bell) pepper, deseeded and diced
225g (8oz) chorizo sausage
2 tsp 'nduja paste
2 x 400g (14oz) tins chopped tomatoes
150g (5½oz) cherry tomatoes
4 medium eggs
1 ball of buffalo mozzarella, sliced into
    1cm (½in) rounds
10g (⅓oz) fresh coriander (cilantro),
    to garnish
20g (¾oz) crumbled feta, to garnish
    (optional)

EQUIPMENT
chopping board—knife—frying pan with a lid (you can cover it in foil if you don't have a lid) —spatula or wooden spoon

MAKE THE SAUCE
Heat the oil in a frying pan over a medium heat, add the onion and garlic and cook for a few minutes until soft, then add the red pepper and the chorizo. Cook for a little longer until the chorizo gets a bit crispy, then add the 'nduja paste and throw in the chopped tomatoes and cherry tomatoes. I always halve the cherry tomatoes before throwing them in, but you don't have to.

TIME FOR THE EGGS
When it's all bubbling and has reached the consistency you want (around 10–15 minutes), using the back of a spoon make four small wells in the sauce, crack your eggs into them and add the slices of mozzarella. Cover with the lid and let it bubble until the eggs are done to your liking. Remove the lid and sprinkle over coriander and feta (if using) to finish. It's great warm on toast and perfect on its own, too.

ALTERNATIVE INGREDIENTS
Red onion: use white or shallots
Red pepper: use orange, yellow or green (but red is sweeter)
'Nduja paste: use chilli or remove the spicy heat all together

'To Cure a Cold' Chicken Ramen

This ramen-style chicken soup is the perfect dish to 'cure a cold'. It's jam-packed with goodness, the ginger and chilli help relieve any sinus congestion, and all the veggies and gentle chicken broth flavours sooth you while giving your body the good kick of nutrients that it needs!

2 skinless chicken breasts
olive or sesame oil
250g (9oz) dried wheat noodles
4 garlic cloves, peeled and finely chopped
2.5cm (1in) piece of ginger, finely chopped
½ fresh red chilli, finely chopped
1–2 tbsp soy sauce
1–2 tbsp tamarind paste
500ml (17fl oz/generous 2 cups) chicken stock (bouillon)
1 or 2 bok choy, sliced
1 carrot, peeled into strips
100g (3½oz) beansprouts
salt and pepper

TO SERVE
1 tbsp finely chopped fresh coriander (cilantro)
2 spring onions (scallions), trimmed and finely chopped
boiled egg (optional) (boil for 6½ minutes for a perfect jammy egg)

EQUIPMENT
chopping board—knife—deep frying pan spoon

COOK THE CHICKEN
Season the chicken breasts with salt and pepper. Heat a little oil in the frying pan over a medium-high heat, add the chicken breasts and cook for 18–20 minutes until they are cooked through and golden on both sides. Remove from the pan and set aside to rest.

COOK THE NOODLES
Cook the noodles according to the packet instructions. Drain.

MAKE THE RAMEN
Heat a little oil in the pan, add the chopped garlic, ginger and chilli and cook for a minute, then add the soy sauce and tamarind. Stir, then pour in the chicken stock. Add your veggies and noodles and bring to the boil, then turn the heat down and simmer for 2 minutes, until the soup is warmed through.

SERVE
Plate up the noodles and veg with lots of that broth. Slice the chicken breasts then plonk them on top along with a garnish of coriander, spring onion and an egg if you like!

ALTERNATIVE INGREDIENTS
Chicken breasts: use firm tofu or king prawns (shrimp), or beef steak (and substitute the chicken stock for beef stock)
Veggies: use broccoli, peas or sweetcorn
Chicken stock (bouillon): use vegetable or beef stock

Family Friday-Night-In Pizzas

My family-night pizzas are a real winner. They taste better than take-out and are more fun to make! If you're looking for something to do with your family on Friday night, look no further: the dough is fluffy and delicious, and you can tailor the toppings to each family member so everyone is happy (I know, read that again!). This is also a wonderful recipe for date night or a friends' night in – make your pizzas in the shape of a heart to surprise your loved ones!

Make the dough up to 24 hours ahead of time and chill until needed, then take it out, give it a roll and make your personalised pizzas.

7g (¼oz) yeast
1 tbsp granulated sugar
350g (12½oz/2½ cups) lukewarm water
450g (1lb/3½ cups) strong white bread
    flour, plus extra for dusting
2 tbsp olive oil, plus extra for greasing
4 tbsp pizza tomato sauce
60g (2¼oz) grated mozzarella
toppings of choice

EQUIPMENT
bowl—whisk—stand mixer fitted with dough hook (optional)—wooden spoon rolling pin—baking tray

MAKE THE DOUGH
Put the yeast and sugar in a bowl and pour over the warm water. Whisk and leave to stand for 5 minutes until frothy, with bubbles on the top. Add the flour and olive oil and mix to form a dough. I use a stand mixer fitted with the dough hook and mix for about 5 minutes. If you don't have a stand mixer, bring the dough together with a wooden spoon then pop it onto a floured surface and knead for 10 minutes or so. If you're using a stand mixer, remove the dough from the mixer bowl after 5 minutes of kneading then knead it by hand: this way you can feel if it needs slightly more flour – you don't want it too wet so it sticks to everything. Put your ball of dough in a greased bowl, cover with a tea towel (dish towel) and leave somewhere warm to double or nearly triple in size for 20–30 minutes.

PREHEAT THE OVEN
Preheat the oven to 200°C (180°C fan/400°F/gas mark 6).

THE FUN PART
Punch the air out of the risen dough and tip it out onto a floured surface. Cut it in half then roll out your dough, place each piece on a baking tray and start making your pizzas. If you like a stuffed crust, put the stuffing you want around the edges then fold the edges in to cover the stuffing. Add your tomato sauce, mozzarella and toppings to the pizzas, pop them in the oven for 10 minutes until they're golden brown, cooked and looking delicious. Slice, serve and enjoy!

ALTERNATIVE INGREDIENTS
Mozzarella: use veggie or vegan mozzarella or remove the cheese completely

Time to Impress – Mushroom & Prosecco Risotto

There were a few years, when I was a teenager, that my mum would request that I made this for every special occasion, whether for a birthday or for friends, and she had good reason. It's creamy, it has indulgent truffle oil, and above all else it has an undertone of prosecco. This is defo one to make when you have people over – it's incredibly simple yet makes you look fancy pants!

4 tbsp truffle oil, plus extra for drizzling
2 shallots, peeled and finely diced
1 bulb of garlic, cloves peeled and finely chopped
500g (1lb 2oz) variety of mushrooms (I like chestnut, portobello and shiitake), sliced
200g (7oz) arborio rice
600ml (20fl oz/2½ cups) prosecco
500ml (17fl oz/generous 2 cups) chicken stock (bouillon)
225g (8oz) parmesan cheese, grated
a handful of fresh chopped chives, plus extra to serve
2 tbsp butter
large pinch of salt (you can use garlic or truffle salt here)
large pinch of freshly ground black pepper

EQUIPMENT
chopping board—knife—grater—deep frying pan—wooden spoon

MAKE THE BASE
Heat the truffle oil in a frying pan over a medium-low heat, add the shallots and garlic and cook for 5 minutes until soft (be careful because the garlic will catch quickly, cook them low and slow).

COOK THE RISOTTO
Add the mushrooms to the pan and cook for 8–10 minutes until they start to shrink and wilt. Add the risotto rice and stir it around for a minute or two then add the prosecco. Simmer for a couple of minutes then add the chicken stock and let it simmer, stirring often, for 6–8 minutes until the rice has soaked up 90 per cent of the liquid. Throw in the parmesan, chives and butter and keep stirring, loosening with more stock if necessary. Your risotto is cooked when it is rich and creamy, and the rice is al dente with a slight bite. Season to taste with the salt and pepper.

SERVE
Remove from the heat and serve, drizzled with a little extra truffle oil and sprinkled with more chopped chives.

ALTERNATIVE INGREDIENTS
Truffle oil: use olive oil or garlic oil (just be aware that the flavour will carry through the dish so something like a sesame oil that has a rather distinct flavour probably wouldn't work here)
Shallots: use onion but I really think that shallots complement this dish beautifully, they're not as potent and are slightly more mild and sweet throughout this dish
Chicken stock (bouillon): use vegetable stock or beef stock

Salmon Dinner
in a Foil Parcel

SERVES 2

My mum and I ate this almost every evening a couple of years ago. I was waitressing and she worked all day too, so we only had minutes to make dinner and we wanted something warming that required minimum effort but would make us feel like we had had a hearty dinner packed with goodness. These little salmon parcels were excellent: we would throw in any veggies that needed eating up, whack in a tin of butter beans or cannellini beans if we were feeling particularly hungry, and in 15 minutes dinner would be done. Make it your own and put your mind at ease knowing your body has been properly nourished and you still have time to do all the other things you need to do.

6–8 asparagus spears, trimmed and
    chopped
3 garlic cloves, peeled and finely chopped
handful of sliced mushrooms
handful of kale leaves, chopped
400g (14oz) tin tomatoes
2 salmon fillets
drizzle of olive oil
squeeze of lemon juice
large pinch each of salt and pepper

EQUIPMENT
chopping board—knife—foil—baking tray

PREHEAT THE OVEN
Preheat the oven to 200°C (180°C fan/400°F/gas mark 6). Place two sheets of foil on a work surface.

ARRANGE THE INGREDIENTS ON THE FOIL
Divide the asparagus, garlic, mushrooms, kale and tinned tomatoes between each piece of foil, placing them in the centre of each sheet, pouring the tomatoes over the vegetables. Place a salmon fillet on top of each pile, drizzle with olive oil squeeze over some lemon juice, and season each fillet with salt and pepper. Fold the foil around each salmon and veggie pile to make a little package.

TIME TO COOK
Pop the packages on a baking tray and bake in the oven for 15 minutes. Remove and unwrap (be careful unwrapping them – you've basically made a mini makeshift steamer, so there will be a lot of steam as you open it). Serve up and enjoy.

ALTERNATIVE INGREDIENTS
Veg: any vegetables you have in the veggie drawer, any tins of beans or packet rice and grains
Salmon: swap for another fish or use chicken or beef (just be aware you may need to adjust the cooking time to make sure the meat is cooked through)

Truffle Mayo
Chicken Sandwich

When I was playing around in the kitchen one day, I found some truffle mayo I'd been given and thought, okay, let's make this chicken sandwich fancy today. I wanted a creamy, saucy sandwich and with the addition of truffle mayo, this deliciousness was created.

2 large ciabatta or panini breads
knob of butter
6 tbsp truffle mayo
1 garlic clove, peeled and finely chopped
30g (1oz) parmesan cheese, finely grated
2 heads of romaine (cos) lettuce, roughly
  chopped
200g (7oz) shredded cooked chicken
  (leftover roast chicken is perfect here)

EQUIPMENT
toaster—chopping board—knife—grater
bowl

TOAST THE BREAD
Toast your bread so it's crispy, then spread on that butter as you would any normal sandwich.

MAKE THE FILLING, ASSEMBLE AND SERVE
Put the mayo, garlic and grated parmesan in a bowl and mix well (this is effectively your dressing). Throw the lettuce in the bowl along with the chicken and mix to coat. Add the filling to the middle of your toasted bread and you're ready to enjoy a deliciously simple, seemingly fancy sandwich!

ALTERNATIVE INGREDIENTS
Truffle mayo: use normal mayo, or light mayo for a lower calorie option
Veggie option: leave out the chicken – the salad, parmesan and truffle mayonnaise is a lovely rich combination.

Messy Sausage Pasta

SERVES 4

I used to whip up this little number at university, especially because for some reason, our local supermarket always had sausages in the 'reduced to clear' section. I make it with chicken sausages, pork sausages and even chorizo – it's delicious every time. Mix up the pasta shapes with your favourite sausage and you have a delicious dinner in under twenty minutes.

400g (14oz) bucatini pasta
knob of butter
6 garlic cloves, peeled and finely chopped
8 sausages (your favourite – I find chicken sausages work brilliantly)
400g (14oz) tin chopped tomatoes
150ml (5fl oz/⅔ cup) single (light) cream
80g (2¾oz) parmesan cheese, grated, plus extra to serve
a handful of chopped basil
salt and pepper

EQUIPMENT
chopping board—knife— grater
saucepan—frying pan—wooden spoon

COOK THE PASTA
Bring a saucepan of salted water to the boil (I add a drizzle of olive oil to my pasta cooking water – some say this does nothing, but I really think it helps flavour the pasta and stops it sticking together), then add the pasta and cook according to the packet instructions.

MAKE THE SAUCE
While the pasta's cooking, melt the butter in the frying pan over a medium-low heat, add the garlic and cook it gently until it is aromatic, making sure it doesn't burn. Cut your sausages into little chunks or squeeze the meat from the casings, add the meat to the pan and break up the meat with the wooden spoon in the pan as it cooks. When the meat is cooked, about 5–8 minutes, add the tomatoes, cream and parmesan and stir until everything is combined. When the sauce is bubbling gently, take it off the heat and stir through most of the basil.

MIX THE PASTA AND SAUCE, THEN SERVE
Add the drained pasta to the sauce; it doesn't matter if some of that pasta water comes with it – it will add extra creaminess to your sauce. Mix the pasta to coat and serve it up, garnished with a little more basil and seasoned with salt and pepper (I always add more parmesan – you can never have enough cheese on pasta in my eyes!).

The pasta and sauce will keep in the fridge in an airtight container for up to 2–3 days.

ALTERNATIVE INGREDIENTS
Pasta: use your favourite pasta shape, perhaps macaroni, fusilli, penne, or you could even use orzo
Butter: as the recipe uses cream and parmesan, I find the most complimentary fat is butter, but you can switch it for olive oil.
Sausages: use chicken or beef mince – it will work just the same as sausage meat
Parmesan: use your favourite cheese (my sister's favourite is Cheddar)

My Momma's Weeknight Favourite – Chicken Caesar Salad

SERVES 4

My mum asks for this every single week. Caesar salad is her favourite meal and she says it's the best she has had (no, she isn't biased – she will tell me when something isn't up to scratch and this constructive criticism is how I make the best Caesar salad!). I know lots of people don't like anchovies (I used to be one of them) but when they are chopped finely throughout the dressing you really can't taste them at all and they bring a lovely element of saltiness to the dish.

1 loaf of ciabatta, cut into small pieces (about the size of the top of your thumb)
5 tbsp olive oil
1 tbsp dried Italian seasoning
1 tsp salt
1 tsp garlic granules
8 tbsp good-quality mayonnaise
1 tbsp white wine vinegar
1 garlic clove, peeled and grated
200g (7oz) parmesan cheese, finely grated
4–6 anchovy fillets in oil, finely chopped (along with some of the oil they're in)
3 romaine (cos) lettuce hearts, roughly chopped
4 cooked chicken thighs or breasts, chopped into bite size pieces

EQUIPMENT
chopping board—knife—grater—large bowl—baking tray—salad servers

PREHEAT THE OVEN AND BAKE THE CROUTONS
Preheat the oven to 200°C (180°C fan/400°F/gas mark 6). Put the ciabatta pieces in a large bowl, drizzle the olive oil over them and add the Italian seasoning, salt and garlic granules. Mix well, lay them out on a baking tray and bake in the oven for about 8 minutes until golden brown (keep an eye on them as they catch quickly). Meanwhile, prepare the salad.

MAKE THE DRESSING
Use the same bowl you seasoned your croutons in (so all the flavour from the croutons that are stuck to the side of the bowl are going to make it into the salad). Add the mayonnaise, vinegar, grated garlic, grated parmesan and chopped anchovies (and a drizzle of the anchovy oil) to the bowl, mixing it well until fully combined.

TOSS THE SALAD
Add the romaine lettuce, cooked chicken, and croutons and mix them really well through the dressing – you want the dressing to kiss every element of that bowl – and that is it.

ALTERNATIVE INGREDIENTS
Chicken: use a light meat like turkey, or even prawns
Italian seasoning: use a mixture of dried basil, oregano and parsley
Romaine (cos) lettuce: use baby gem, or if you're looking for a leaf with a little more nutrients go for darker coloured leaves and bags of salad (you just miss out on the crunch that the romaine brings)
Anchovies: use fish sauce, Worcestershire sauce, chopped bacon, green olives or chopped capers

Tomato & Spinach Tortellini Bake

This recipe is a dream to make. It's veggie and warming, and the little tortellini mouthfuls offer bags of flavour. A pasta dish is like a hug and with this cheese pasta bake scattered with spinach and tomatoes you get nutrition with every bite!

knob of butter
1 white onion, peeled and finely diced
250g (9oz) fresh plum tomatoes
500g (1lb 2oz) tortellini (choose your favourite – I like 3-cheese or ricotta and spinach)
2 tbsp tomato puree (paste)
500ml (17fl oz/generous 2 cups) double (heavy) cream
80g (2¾oz) parmesan cheese, grated, plus extra to serve
2–3 large handfuls of spinach
80g (2¾oz) mature (sharp) Cheddar cheese, grated
basil, to serve (optional)

EQUIPMENT
chopping board—knife—grater—frying pan—saucepan—large ovenproof dish (optional)

MAKE THE SAUCE
Melt the butter in the frying pan over a medium heat, throw in the onion and plum tomatoes and cook for 5 minutes or so – you want the tomatoes to blister and reduce down to a lovely sweet sauce. Add the tomato puree, cream, parmesan and spinach, reduce the heat to low and let the sauce to just bubble away for 2–3 minutes, until it has thickened.

TIME FOR THE PASTA
Meanwhile, cook the tortellini in a saucepan of boiling water for a couple of minutes (according to the packet instructions). Spoon your little pasta parcels into the creamy tomato sauce (if your frying pan can go in the oven, sprinkle the top with the Cheddar cheese and whack it under the grill until the cheese is golden and bubbling). If it can't, just transfer the pasta and sauce to the ovenproof dish, sprinkle in the Cheddar cheese and grill until golden and bubbling.

SERVE
Spoon the tortellini and sauce onto plates and enjoy!

The dish will keep in the fridge for 2–3 days.

ALTERNATIVE INGREDIENTS
Spinach: use broccoli florets
Double (heavy) cream: use single (light) cream or cream cheese here, or a vegan alternative

One-pan Orzo Salmon

SERVES 4

It can be hard coming up with new material for mid-week meals, whether that's to feed yourself, you and your partner, or the whole family. This one-pan wonder has everything: lots of veggies, carbs and healthy fats. It will keep you feeling full and satisfied, and who doesn't love to whip up a dish they can enjoy the next day for lunch or dinner?

3–4 tbsp olive oil
a handful of fresh parsley, finely chopped
6 garlic cloves, peeled and finely chopped
3–4 tbsp lemon juice
4 salmon fillets (skin on or off – your preference)
400g (14oz) orzo
a bunch of asparagus, trimmed and cut into bite-sized pieces
half a head of broccoli, cut into bite-sized pieces
150g (5½oz) peas
600ml (20fl oz/2½ cups) chicken or vegetable stock (bouillon)
150g (5½oz) parmesan cheese, grated
200g (7oz) fresh prawns (shrimp), peeled and deveined
4 lemon slices
a few toasted pine nuts
salt and pepper

EQUIPMENT
chopping board—knife— grater— large pan with a lid (you can cover it in foil if you don't have a lid)—wooden spoon

MARINATE THE SALMON
Preheat your oven to 200°C (180°C fan/400°F/gas mark 6). Put the oil, finely chopped parsley, garlic and lemon juice in the large pan you're going to cook the orzo in. Mix well, coat your salmon fillets in the mixture then set them aside.

TIME FOR THE PASTA
Put the orzo in the pan with the chopped vegetables, peas and stock. Mix to ensure the orzo doesn't stick to the bottom of the pan and the herbs and vegetables are all mixed in evenly. Cover with the lid and pop it in the oven for 15 minutes (if you need to mix occasionally that's fine – you don't want the orzo catching on the bottom of the pan).

ADD THE SALMON
Remove the dish from the oven and mix through the grated parmesan and the prawns. Place the marinated salmon on top and season with salt and pepper. Add the lemon slices, replace the lid and pop it in the oven for another 8–10 minutes: at this point the salmon will be cooked perfectly.

SERVE
Remove from the oven, sprinkle with the pine nuts and any other leftover herbs and enjoy!

ALTERNATIVE INGREDIENTS
Salmon: use another meaty fish such as halibut or tuna
Herbs: any fresh herbs, such as dill, chives, sage, rosemary, mint or even bay leaves
Broccoli and asparagus: use green beans, Brussels sprouts, artichokes... the options are endless
Parmesan: use feta for a more summery dish
Prawns (shrimp): use mussels or calamari rings

Creamy Pan-seared Salmon

SERVES 4

My nana buys fresh fish every Monday from 'Mark, the fish man'. She has been doing this for us for the last 15 years, and we've had salmon every Monday for 15 years, so I've had time to come up with some of the tastiest salmon recipes around! This creamy salmon on a bed of fluffy rice is utterly gorgeous, creamy comfort food.

4 salmon fillets, skin on or off, it's up to you
1 tsp salt
1 tsp freshly ground black pepper
1 tsp garlic granules
2 tbsp olive oil
500g (1lb 2oz) mascarpone
grated zest and juice of 2 lemons
60g (2¼oz) capers, chopped
a large handful of chopped parsley
a few lemon slices, to serve

EQUIPMENT
chopping board—knife— grater or zester
large frying pan—whisk

SEAR THE SALMON
Season the salmon fillets generously on both sides with the salt, pepper and garlic granules. Heat the oil in a large frying pan over a medium heat then add the salmon fillets and sear on each side for 2 minutes (so a total of 8 minutes for searing both pieces at the same time). Remove from the pan and set aside.

MAKE THE CREAMY LEMON SAUCE
Add the mascarpone to the pan (so it combines with all that flavour from searing the salmon) along with the lemon zest and juice, capers and parsley (I sometimes add a splash of the caper brine too), whisk it all together in the pan to fully combine.

FINISHING TOUCHES
When the sauce has a thick consistency and starts to bubble slightly, add the seared salmon and tuck the fillets into that sauce. Top with lemon slices and a little more parsley to serve.

ALTERNATIVE INGREDIENTS
Salmon: use a meaty fish like a halibut or hake. If you're not a fish person, use chicken, but take into account the additional cooking time.
Mascarpone: use something that will loosen up when heated but keep its creamy consistency, such as a cream cheese or ricotta, but remember ricotta has a slightly stronger flavour
Capers: use chopped green olives, pickles or even anchovies (you want that saltiness)

Speedy Creamy Chicken Risotto

SERVES 2

Welcome to my speedy risotto! I sometimes worry people think risotto is a technical, time-intensive dish – I've read so many recipes that require you to lay the risotto rice out on a tray and cool it, or have other steps that don't make it speedy. This recipe keeps it simple. If you have people coming over and want to make it fancy pants, add a little Prosecco or Champagne and drizzle it in truffle oil! It's a versatile dish that can be elevated for any event.

25g (1oz) butter
1 white onion, peeled and finely diced
6–8 garlic cloves, peeled and finely chopped
150g (5½oz) risotto rice
150ml (5fl oz/⅔ cup) white wine
350ml (12fl oz/1½ cups) chicken stock (bouillon)
125g (4¼oz) shredded cooked chicken (leftover roast chicken is perfect here)
125g (4¼oz) parmesan cheese, grated
salt and pepper

TO SERVE
basil leaves
olive oil, for drizzling

EQUIPMENT
chopping board—knife—grater
saucepan or frying pan with a lid—wooden spoon

COOK THE ONION AND GARLIC
Melt the butter in a saucepan or frying pan over a low heat, add the onion and garlic and cook for 5 minutes until soft, translucent, and on their way to being caramelised (you really want to engage with the sweetness here).

ADD THE RICE
Stir the risotto rice into the pan, then add the wine and chicken stock. Cover with a lid and cook for 10–11 minutes (you want the rice to be cooked but still have a slight bite, so it doesn't go mushy). Remove from the heat and stir through the chicken and parmesan (this makes it creamy and thick). Season to taste.

SERVE
It really is that simple. Serve and enjoy, topped with basil leaves and a drizzle of olive oil.

ALTERNATIVE INGREDIENTS
Butter: use olive oil, or any form of fat.
White wine: use Prosecco or Champagne, or if you can't drink or use alcohol in cooking, you can swap this for the same quantity of stock
Chicken stock (bouillon): to make this veggie, use vegetable stock
Chicken: to make this veggie, add other veggies when you're cooking the onion and garlic, such as mushrooms, sweet potatoes, leeks or butternut squash. Most veggies work well here.
Parmesan cheese: the parmesan helps make the dish creamy and gives it a nutty bite, but it can be swapped for 100ml (3½fl oz/scant ½ cup) of cream of your choice
Garnish: use any fresh herb you have, or just keep it simple with a crack of black pepper. To make this fancy pants for guests or a date night, or you're wanting to treat yourself after a long week, try truffle oil – it works beautifully!

COMFORT

in 30

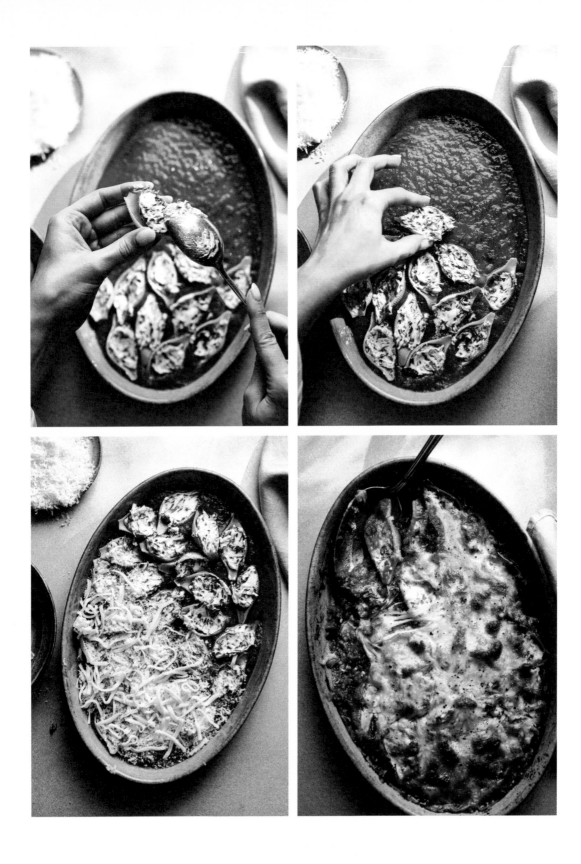

Ricotta-stuffed Tomato Pasta

This recipe was a happy accident: I bought some large pasta shells and used some bits and bobs that I had at home to fill them which resulted in this dish. I loved it and after a few more trial runs I perfected it. I always loved stuffed ricotta and spinach in a tortellini and love tomato-based pasta dishes: put two and two together and you get stuffed cheesy pasta shapes with the tomato sauce. Win, win!

600g (1lb 5oz) your favourite tomato-based sauce (one with lots of flavour – I love an Italian one infused with lots of garlic and basil)
250g (9oz) ricotta
2 handfuls of spinach leaves, roughly chopped
2 tsp garlic granules
1 tsp freshly ground black pepper
280g (9¾oz) large conchiglioni pasta
100g (3½oz) parmesan cheese, grated
100g (3½oz) grated mozzarella
salt

EQUIPMENT
chopping board—knife—grater—large baking dish—medium bowl—spoon

PREHEAT THE OVEN AND STUFF THE PASTA SHAPES
Preheat the oven to 200°C (180°C fan/400°F/gas mark 6). Pop the tomato sauce in a large baking dish. Put the ricotta and chopped spinach in a bowl along with the garlic granules, pepper and season to taste with the salt then give it a good mix. Grab your big pasta shapes, spoon the ricotta mixture into each one and place them firmly in the tomato sauce so they are buried in it (this helps the pasta soften in the oven).

BAKE THE PASTA
Sprinkle the grated cheeses evenly over the top of the dish, cover with foil and bake in the oven for 20 minutes, then remove the foil and let the cheese bubble and become golden for another 10 minutes. Serve and enjoy.

ALTERNATIVE INGREDIENTS
Conchiglioni pasta: use any of your favourite pasta shapes that are big enough to stuff. I sometimes use large rigatoni.
Ricotta: use any soft cheese. Mascarpone works really well, or soft cheeses flavoured with garlic and herbs.
Parmesan and mozzarella: use your favourite kind of cheese, maybe Cheddar, or even blue cheese!

Lamb Pitta Koftas

There is something about lamb koftas that makes them perfect all year round, whether it's spring when lamb is in season, summer with fresh salads and dips, autumn with warm hummus and pitta breads, or winter bejewelled with juicy pomegranate seeds and cranberries. The warm flavours and spices make it a meal to remember with friends and family!

FOR THE KOFTAS
500g (1lb 2oz) minced (ground) lamb
1 onion, peeled and grated
4 garlic cloves, peeled and grated
a handful of parsley, finely chopped,
    plus extra to serve
30g (1oz) breadcrumbs
1 medium egg
1 fresh red chilli, finely chopped
2 tsp ground cumin
2 tsp ground coriander
2 tsp paprika
1 tsp cinnamon
1 tsp cayenne pepper
1 tsp salt

FOR THE TZATZIKI
(optional) – or use shop-bought tzatziki
6 tbsp full fat Greek yoghurt
2 garlic cloves, peeled and grated
½ cucumber, cored and grated
a small handful of dill, finely chopped
juice of 1 lemon, plus extra to serve
pinch of salt

TO SERVE
4 x flatbreads
40g (1¼oz) feta, crumbled

PREHEAT THE OVEN AND MAKE THE KOFTAS
Preheat the oven to 200°C (180°C fan/400°F/gas mark 6). To one of the large bowls add the lamb mince, grated onion and garlic, chopped parsley, breadcrumbs, egg and all the seasonings. Get your hands in there and give it a good mix together so everything is incorporated, then make little sausage shapes with the mixture and lay them on a baking tray and bake in the oven for 15 minutes until browned and cooked through.

IF YOU'RE MAKING HOMEMADE TZATZIKI
Put the Greek yoghurt, grated garlic, grated cucumber, dill, lemon juice and salt in a bowl, give it a good mix and that's it done!

SERVE
Spread the tzatziki on the flatbreads and place the cooked koftas on top. Sprinkle on feta and parsley and enjoy!

ALTERNATIVE INGREDIENTS
Minced lamb: use another kind of mince
Spices: play around with spices in your cupboard, just remember if you're a beginner cook add a little at a time and don't go mad – it's easier to add seasoning than it is to take it out!

EQUIPMENT
chopping board—knife—grater—2 large bowls—baking tray

Pan-seared Sea Bass
with Crispy Chorizo Mash

This sea bass with crispy chorizo mash is the perfect dinner for two and a great way to impress – it's a lazy dish that looks like you've put so much more effort into it than you have. Crispy fish combined with a garlicky mash scattered with little salty pieces of chorizo... it makes you salivate just thinking about it!

4 sea bass fillets
4 tsp butter
1 lemon, halved
salt and pepper
a handful of chopped parsley, to serve

FOR THE GARLICKY CHORIZO MASH
1 bulb of garlic
olive oil, for drizzling
1kg (2lb 4oz) floury potatoes (I like to peel
    them), cut into similar-sized chunks
50g (1¾oz) butter
50–100ml (1¾–3½fl oz/scant ¼ –scant
    ½ cup) whole (full-fat) milk
250g (9oz) cooking chorizo, chopped into
    1.5cm (½in) cubes

EQUIPMENT
chopping board—knife—foil—large
saucepan—masher—frying pan—tongs

ALTERNATIVE INGREDIENTS
Chorizo: use pancetta
Milk: use the same quantity of single (light) cream

PREHEAT THE OVEN AND PREP THE FANCY-PANTS GARLIC
Preheat the oven to 200°C (180°C fan/400°F/gas mark 6). To confit the garlic (trust me, it sounds so much fancier than it is, but now you can say 'I know how to confit garlic'!), cut the top off the garlic bulb and place it on a sheet of foil. Drizzle olive oil all over the bulb, to cover each clove in oil, wrap the bulb in foil and pop it in the oven while you cook everything else.

POTATO TIME!
Cook the potato chunks in a saucepan of boiling water for 20 minutes, until cooked – if you stab one with a sharp knife it should fall off on its own. Strain, pop back into the saucepan, add the butter, a pinch of salt and lots of crushed black pepper and mash, then add 50ml (1¾fl oz/scant ¼ cup) of the milk and keep mashing. If it's still a little dry, keep adding milk until it's the consistency you like!

COOK THE CHORIZO AND SEA BASS
While the potatoes are cooking, season the fish on both sides with salt and pepper. Set aside. Place the frying pan over a medium heat, throw in the chorizo and cook for 5 minutes until crisped up and those delicious oils have been released! Throw into the mash and mix through (pour in some of that chorizo fat too). Melt the butter in the pan that the chorizo was in and when it starts to bubble, add the sea bass. Cook for 3 minutes on one side, then flip it to cook on the other side, squeeze over the lemon and let the sea bass cook in the lemon juice for a further 3 minutes. It should be perfectly golden brown on each side.

REMEMBER THAT GARLIC?
Remove the garlic from the oven (it will be hot, so be careful or use oven gloves) and squeeze the soft and creamy garlic cloves out of the bulb. Mix these through the mash.

SERVE
Serve portions of mash topped with sea bass and a sprinkle of parsley to finish.

COMFORT IN 30 **97**

One-pan Apple & Pork Dinner

SERVES 2

Pork chops get a bad rep as slightly bland and boring, but a countryside supper isn't complete without a little cider and pork. This one-pan dinner is so easy and fuss-free, and it looks delicious and tastes even better. It's also not too heavy, though as autumn and winter come around it really does warm the soul. Serve it with whatever you fancy, I find a hearty mash is always a winner in our household.

3–4 tbsp olive oil
4 bone-in pork chops
large knob of butter
1 red onion, peeled and thinly sliced
1 gala apple, peeled, cored and
   thickly sliced
6 garlic cloves, peeled and finely chopped
a few sprigs of fresh sage
a few sprigs of fresh rosemary
150–200ml (5–7fl oz/⅔–generous ¾ cup)
   apple cider of your choice
salt and pepper

EQUIPMENT
chopping board—knife—deep, large frying pan—spoon or tongs

COOK THOSE CHOPS
Drizzle the oil over the pork chops and season with a large pinch each of salt and pepper. Place the frying pan over a medium-high heat, add the pork chops and cook for about 5 minutes on each side until golden brown (don't worry about cooking them through completely). Set aside.

CIDER TIME
Add the butter to the pan, reduce the heat to medium, throw in the onion, apple and garlic and cook for 5 minutes until soft. Put the chops back in the pan along with the sprigs of herbs, pour in the cider and cook until the alcohol has cooked off, about 1 minute, then simmer for 5 more minutes until the pork chops are cooked through.

SERVE
Remove from the heat and serve.

ALTERNATIVE INGREDIENTS
Cider: use apple juice or chicken or vegetable stock

Sunday Sports
Chicken Mac 'n' Cheese

Honestly this is one of the cosiest dinners you can make! Mac 'n' cheese, the slow-moving carb fest, is the king of comfort food and the ultimate dish to sit on the sofa with and relax while watching your favourite film (my go-to is Harry Potter). It's not supposed to be healthy but it is supposed to put smiles on faces! It's the perfect thing to make for a friend who's having a rubbish time, or for your other half if they've had a hard week at work. Make it on a Sunday afternoon, sit down and eat together. After all, that's what mac 'n' cheese is for... and if it's been a REALLY tough week, head to the drink pairing section and crack that bottle open too.

3 skinless and boneless chicken breasts, cut into thin strips (or leftover Sunday roast chicken)

seasoning of your choice (I keep it simple with a mixture of salt, pepper, garlic granules and paprika but use whatever you have in the cupboard)

450g (1lb) macaroni

3 tbsp butter

3 tbsp plain (all-purpose) flour

300ml (10fl oz/1¼ cups) whole (full-fat) milk

250g (9oz) garlic and herb cream cheese

250ml (8fl oz/1 cup) double (heavy) cream

125g (4¼oz) mature (sharp) Cheddar cheese, grated

COOK THE CHICKEN (IF NOT USING LEFTOVER CHICKEN)
Season the chicken strips and sear in a hot frying pan for 5–7 minutes until they have picked up some colour and are cooked through. Pop the chicken in a bowl and set aside.

PREHEAT THE OVEN
Preheat your oven to 200°C (180°C fan/400°F/gas mark 6).

COOK THE PASTA AND MAKE THE SAUCE
Put your pasta on to boil in a large saucepan of well-salted water and then you can get the sauce sorted. Melt the butter in the pan you cooked the chicken in (if cooking it from scratch) over a medium heat then add the flour and mix it to form a paste. Gradually add the milk, whisking continuously, until it starts to thicken, then add the garlic and herb cream cheese, whisking until fully combined. Add the cream and three quarters of the grated cheese (90–100g (3¼-3½oz) of each cheese) and keep mixing the sauce until it begins to thicken.

ASSEMBLE THE DISH
When the sauce is thick and cheesy add the drained al dente pasta and mix it through. The sauce gets stuck in all the tubes of the macaroni which is just what we want. Stir in the chicken pieces then pour the pasta, sauce and chicken into your baking dish and sprinkle all of the remaining cheese on top (if you have want a crunchy topping, just crumble the crisps over the cheese).

recipe continued

125g (4¼oz) red Leicester, grated
125g (4¼oz) Jarlsberg, grated
125g (4¼oz) grated mozzarella
salt and pepper
cheesy tortilla crisps or cheese puffs, for
   topping (optional)

EQUIPMENT
chopping board—knife—grater—2 large
saucepans—whisk—bowl—large baking
dish

BAKE THE MACARONI CHEESE
Pop the dish in the oven and wait for the cheese to be melted
and golden and the sides to be bubbling, this should take around
10 minutes. Dig into that treasure trove of golden carby pasta
goodness, this is one of the cosiest dinners you can make! It's not
supposed to be healthy, but it will put smiles on the faces of the
people you serve it to.

ALTERNATIVE INGREDIENTS
Whole milk: use semi-skimmed milk (it will just take longer to reduce)
Chicken: use sausages, turkey or beef strips
Garlic and herb cream cheese: use plain cream cheese – the garlic just
adds slightly more flavour – or use mascarpone or cottage cheese
Cheeses: experiment with a favourite cheese or if double up on one you
already have

Burrito Burger

When I went to Oklahoma to visit family, I saw burgers and burritos on a menu and couldn't decide which to have. I thought, why can't I have a burrito burger? This combines all the best bits about burgers – the bun, patty and cheese – with my favourite bits of a burrito – the black beans, guac and pico de gallo. When you have friends over for a barbecue, it's worth making these. Prep a lot of it in advance and it'll just take two minutes to assemble. You can make the patties ahead of time and chill for up to 2 days (or freeze the patties for up to 3 months and defrost before cooking).

4 brioche burger buns
4 cheese slices (I use a Mexican-style jalapeño and chilli one)
200g (7oz) refried black beans, warmed through to serve

FOR THE PATTIES
600g (1lb 5oz) minced (ground) beef (the higher % fat, the juicer your burger – I use 15% fat)
1 tsp salt
1 tsp freshly ground black pepper
2 tsp garlic granules or powder

FOR THE PICO DE GALLO
1 white onion, peeled and finely diced
4 large tomatoes, finely diced
a handful of fresh coriander (cilantro), finely chopped
juice of 1 lime
large pinch of salt

MAKE THE PATTIES
Put the mince, salt, pepper and garlic granules or powder in a bowl and mix together really well with your hands. Separate the mince into four equal portions and mould into patties as thick or thin as you wish. Keep in the fridge while you prepare everything else.

MAKE THE PICO DE GALLO
Put the onion, tomatoes and coriander in a bowl, squeeze over the lime juice and add the salt. Mix well and pop to one side – it should be left to sit ideally for 5–15 minutes.

GUAC, GUAC, GUAC
Put the avocado, red onion and coriander in a bowl, squeeze over the lime juice and add the salt. Mix well (mix it longer if you like a smoother guac, but I quite enjoy mine chunky).

MAKE THE CHIPOTLE MAYO
Mix the mayo and chipotle paste in a bowl.

TOAST THE BURGER BUNS AND COOK THE PATTIES
Toast the burger buns for a minute or two on each side in a griddle pan (bear in mind brioche buns are higher in sugar than regular burger buns, so can burn quicker). Set aside then cook the patties for 2 minutes on each side. On the final flip put the cheese slices on top and allow to cook and melt.

recipe continued

FOR THE GUACAMOLE

3 ripe avocados, halved, stoned, peeled
    and diced
½ red onion, peeled and finely chopped
a small handful of fresh coriander
    (cilantro), finely chopped
juice of 1 lime
pinch of salt

FOR THE CHIPOTLE MAYONNAISE

4 tbsp mayonnaise
2 tsp chipotle seasoning or purée

EQUIPMENT

4 bowls—spoon—chopping board—knife
griddle pan

BRING EVERYTHING TOGETHER

While your patties are cooking, layer up your buns. I like to pop the
mayo on the bottom, and then the refried beans, then the patty,
then my guac, pico de gallo and another layer of the mayo on the
top of the bun. That is it – utterly delicious!

ALTERNATIVE INGREDIENTS

Beef mince: use a drained 400g (14oz) tin of black beans with the same
seasoning, and mush them until you have a paste consistency but can
still see chunks of beans. Form into patties (throw in 1–2 tablespoons
of breadcrumbs if the mixture is a little wet) - also feel free to add 1
teaspoon ground cumin and ½ teaspoon of smoked paprika.

Stuffed Meatballs on a Bed of Orzo

SERVES 4

Is there anything more comforting than pasta and meatballs? We have grown up romanticising the dish thanks to Disney films, and our favourite Italian restaurants, and there is something about it that makes you feel like you should be sharing it with your loved ones. It's an easy one to make for unexpected guests, or just on a random Wednesday.

You can prep the meatballs up to 24 hours in advance and refrigerate, or freeze for about 3 months (defrost before cooking).

FOR THE MEATBALLS
500g (1lb 2oz) minced (ground) meat of choice (a 50/50 mix of beef and pork mince works well)
1 tsp garlic granules
1 tsp dried mixed herbs
1 tsp fresh basil
½ tsp salt
½ tsp ground black pepper
200g (7oz) mozzarella, cut into small chunks

FOR THE SAUCE
1 tbsp olive oil
1 red onion, peeled and finely diced
1 bulb of garlic, peeled and finely chopped
4 tbsp tomato purée (paste)
400g (14oz) orzo
2 x 400g (14oz) tins chopped tomatoes
300ml (10fl oz/1¼ cups) beef stock (bouillon)
fresh basil leaves, to serve
parmesan cheese, grated, to serve

EQUIPMENT
chopping board—knife—large bowl
frying pan—wooden spoon-grater

MAKE THE MEATBALLS
Put the mince in the large bowl and add the garlic granules, mixed herbs, basil, salt and pepper. Mix everything together with your hands. Put about a tablespoon of mince in the palm of one of your hands, press a chunk of cheese into the mince and roll the meat around it (so the cheese is in the centre of the meatball). Set aside then repeat with the rest of the mince and cheese.

FRY THE MEATBALLS
Heat the oil for the sauce in the frying pan over a medium heat, add the meatballs and sear for a few minutes until golden brown and slightly crispy (they do not need to be cooked all of the way through). If your pan is too crowded, cook in batches to ensure that the meatballs are crispy. Set aside.

TIME TO GET SAUCY
Add the onion and garlic to the frying pan (add a drizzle more olive oil here if you like) and cook over a medium heat for a couple of minutes until soft. Stir in the tomato purée then add the orzo, chopped tomatoes and beef stock. Stir so the orzo is covered in the liquid, place the meatballs back in, cover with a lid and cook for 8 minutes until the orzo is cooked (it might need a few more minutes, or a little extra stock added, until it's the consistency you want).

SERVE
Garnish with basil, sprinkle with grated parmesan and serve.

ALTERNATIVE INGREDIENTS
Minced (ground) meat: use beef, chicken, turkey, pork... the options are endless
Herbs: I've gone for Italian flavours, but you could use onion powder, parsley or paprika
Mozzarella: use Jarlsberg
Beef stock (bouillon): use any other stock

Baked Garlic & Parsley Crumb Halibut Bites

SERVES 4

This is such a delicious and warming dinner. Everyone loves a baked dish encased in breadcrumbs and garlic – there is something about it that makes you feel cosy inside. Enjoy these bites with a side of my Rustic New Potatoes (see page 139). They also work well on a bed of rice and a squeeze of sweet chilli jam, which is a family favourite.

70g (2½oz) breadcrumbs
70g (2½oz) parmesan cheese, finely grated
a handful of chopped parsley
6 garlic cloves, peeled and grated
1 tsp salt
1 tsp freshly ground black pepper
2 halibut fillets, cut into bite-sized pieces
lemon wedges, to serve
basmati rice or Rustic New Potatoes (see
     page 139), to serve (optional)

EQUIPMENT
grater—chopping board—knife—baking
tray—baking parchment—bowl

PREHEAT THE OVEN AND MAKE THE CRUMB
Preheat the oven to 180°C (160°C fan/350°F/gas mark 4) and line the baking tray with baking parchment. Mix the breadcrumbs, parmesan, parsley, garlic, salt and pepper in a bowl.

COAT THE HALIBUT
Roll the halibut pieces in the breadcrumb mixture to coat (for extra crispiness, do this process twice) and place on the lined baking tray.

BAKE THE BITES
Bake the bites in the oven for 10–15 minutes until those breadcrumbs are golden and crispy!

Serve with lemon wedges and buttery new potatoes or rice.

ALTERNATIVE INGREDIENTS
Halibut: use any meaty fish, such as salmon, cod, hake or haddock (just be aware that when these kinds of fish are cooked, they flake, so don't handle them too much or they may fall apart). When I was at university, I made this with chicken to make chicken nuggets – throw some garlic and parsley in breadcrumbs and there you have it! A kids' tea suitable for adults!
The crumb: throughout this book you'll notice I often say 'have a play' – this recipe is great for playing around with herbs and spices (in my opinion there is no wrong or right way of cooking, if you like a combination of foods together - make it. Food is supposed to make a particular individual feel happy. If you like a kick of heat, throw in some paprika, cayenne pepper or chilli flakes, or if you have a bag of crisps in the cupboard, crush them up and use them instead of breadcrumbs. Cooking is supposed to be easy and stress free, so have a play and enjoy.

Creamy White Wine & Tarragon Chicken

You may have noticed by now that simple recipes are my favourite. I love throwing everything in one pan and muddling it together to create something that makes you warm and cosy inside! This white wine and chicken dish is a fab one, I like to serve it over mashed potatoes for some extra stodgy goodness.

4 skinless chicken breasts
knob of butter
1 onion, peeled and finely diced
6 garlic cloves, peeled and finely chopped
100g (3½oz) green beans, trimmed and cut into 2.5cm (1in) chunks
150ml (5fl oz/⅔ cup) single (light) cream
1 glass of white wine (about 180ml/6fl oz/¾ cup – feel free to pour yourself a glass here too)
150ml (5fl oz/⅔ cup) chicken stock (bouillon)
a small handful of fresh tarragon, finely chopped
salt and pepper

EQUIPMENT
chopping board—knife—large frying pan and lid—tongs—wooden spoon

COOK THE CHICKEN
Season the chicken with salt and pepper. Melt the butter in the frying pan over a medium heat, and sear the chicken breasts on each side until golden, slightly crisp and cooked through. Remove from the pan.

GET SAUCY THEN SERVE
Throw the onion and garlic into the pan and cook for a couple of minutes, then add the green beans and cook for a minute or two in the garlicky butter. Add the cream, white wine, chicken stock, tarragon and a large pinch of sea salt and mix everything together until you have a thick sauce. Return the chicken breasts to the pan, cover the pan with a lid and cook for 20 minutes until the chicken is cooked through. Serve!

The dish will keep in the fridge for up to 3 days, and in the freezer for up to 3 months.

ALTERNATIVE INGREDIENTS
Butter: use olive oil or any other fat
Chicken breasts: use the same weight of turkey breast or another light, white meat (white fish also works well – it's been tried and tested!)
Green beans: swap out for peas, asparagus, broccoli or spinach
Tarragon: basil or rosemary also work well but I really recommend using tarragon if it's available
White wine: use an additional 180ml (6fl oz/¾ cup) of stock (chicken or vegetable will do)

Rainy Day Tomato Soup
with Cheesyyy Toastie

Curling up in an armchair with the fire on and tucking into a hearty soup and crispy cheese toastie is one of my absolute favourite things to do! As autumn approaches, this is the best soup to make when you start to feel the sniffles set in. When I worked in the Alps, this was one of the first things I made for my guests: it satisfies you when it's cold, snowing, blowing a gale or just a bit grey and miserable.

FOR THE SOUP

800g (1lb 12oz) fresh tomatoes (brownie points if they're homegrown), roughly chopped
2 large white onions, peeled and quartered
2 bulbs of garlic, tops cut off
6 tbsp olive oil, plus extra for drizzling
large pinch of salt
good crack of black pepper
400ml (14fl oz/1¾ cups) vegetable stock (bouillon)
1 large tbsp cream cheese
10g (¼oz) basil, torn, to serve

FOR THE TOASTIE

8-12 slices of sourdough bread
a generous spreading of salted butter
100-150g (3½-5½oz) extra mature (super sharp) Cheddar cheese, grated
40-60g (1½-2¼oz) grated mozzarella
Tabasco or hot sauce, to taste

EQUIPMENT
chopping board—knife—baking tray
saucepan—jug blender or stick blender
griddle pan or toastie maker

PREHEAT THE OVEN AND ROAST THE TOMATOES
Preheat the oven to 220°C (200°C fan/425°F/gas mark 7). Put the chopped tomatoes on the baking tray, along with the onion and bulbs of garlic, and drizzle with the olive oil (making sure to douse the garlic bulbs in it – when the oil gets into that bulb and goes into the oven the garlic caramelises, loses its intensity and just gives a hum to the entire dish). Sprinkle over the salt and pepper and shove it in the oven for 15–20 minutes. Basically, you want the tomatoes to blister , the onion to brown and the garlic to squeeze out of its bulb gently without much force.

TIME TO GET SOUPY
Remove the roasted tomatoes, onions and garlic from the oven, put the tomatoes and onions in the saucepan and squeeze the roasted garlic from its skins. Add the silky juices from the roasting tray, then add the stock and cream cheese. Place the pan over a medium heat for a few minutes until warm through then blend the soup to the consistency that you like (I like mine super smooth until there are no bits left).

MAKE THE TOASTIE
Heat a griddle pan over a medium heat (or a toastie maker). Get your favourite cheese, you don't have to use Cheddar and mozzarella but for a simple toastie they're my personal champion cheeses. Butter the outside of two pieces of sourdough. On one of the sides you haven't buttered add your hot sauce, then place your cheese and the other piece of bread, buttered side facing up. Pop in the griddle pan and keep flipping the toastie to ensure an evenly cooked and melted toastie – you want it to be golden and crispy!

SERVE
Finish the soup with a drizzle of olive oil and garnish of basil. Now dunk that toastie in your soup and curl up with your favourite film!

The soup will keep in the fridge for 2–3 days, and in the freezer for up to 3 months.

Skiing Steak
Frites

When I was working in the Alps, steak frites in the mountains was a specialty. There is something about skiing all day, and being slightly wet, cold and damp, that makes you crave chips and meat. When I think of skiing, this is one of my go-to dishes: thinly cut potatoes like potato straws, sprinkled with crunchy sea salt, and succulent steak, with a chimichurri sauce on top. Ohhhh, it's a winner.

400–500ml (14-17fl oz/1¾–generous
   2 cups) vegetable or sunflower oil,
   for frying
2 large rib-eye steaks, at room temperature
2 large Maris Piper or russet potatoes
olive oil, for rubbing the steaks
large knob of butter
3–4 garlic cloves, peeled and bashed
sea salt flakes and freshly ground black
   pepper

FOR THE CHIMICHURRI SAUCE
a handful of parsley, finely chopped
½ red chilli, finely chopped
3–4 cloves roasted garlic (see page 97) (or
   1 regular clove, peeled and chopped)
1 tsp red wine vinegar
pinch of salt
2 tbsp olive oil

EQUIPMENT
chopping board—knife—heavy-based saucepan—slotted spoon—skillet or griddle pan

HEAT THE OIL FOR THE CHIPS
Heat the oil in the saucepan slowly over a medium-low heat. Don't rush, and please be careful!

GET THOSE CHIPS READY!
While the oil is heating up, peel and cut the potatoes into really thin chips (this means they take longer to fry and are going to be crispier on the outside).

FRY THE CHIPS
You can tell whether the oil is hot enough by dipping a chip in it: if it starts to fizz it's ready, if it boils turn down the heat and wait for it to get to the right temperature. Add some chips to the oil and fry for 4–5 minutes until golden brown. Remove with a slotted spoon and leave to drain in kitchen paper to soak up the excess oil, then sprinkle with sea salt. Repeat until you have used up all of the chips. Cover and place in the oven set to a low temperature.

COOK THE STEAKS
Rub the steaks with olive oil and season each with a generous pinch of salt and pepper (on both sides). Put the butter in the skillet or griddle pan along with the garlic and place over a medium-high heat. Make sure the pan is hot – you want to sear the steak, not boil it in the butter – and pop the steaks in the pan. I like my steak rare, so cook them for 1 minute on each side, but feel free to cook it to your preferred level of doneness. When you've turned the steaks once to sear on both sides, continuously baste them in the garlic butter and steak juices. To sear the fat to make it crispy and flavourful, lean the steaks up against the side of the pan. Remove the steaks from the pan after 3–4 minutes (or longer, if you wish: allow 5 minutes for medium rare, 6 for medium) and allow them to rest for the same amount of time.

recipe continued

WHIP UP THE SAUCE

While the steaks rest, combine the sauce ingredients in a bowl.

SERVE

Lay the chips on a plate, slice your steak and lay it over the top. Dollop your chimichurri along the middle of the steak, add one more crack of salt if you like, serve and enjoy.

ALTERNATIVE INGREDIENTS

Potatoes: use any large white potato or sweet potato
Steak: use sirloin, tuna steak, or griddled aubergine (eggplant) or cauliflower for vegetarians or vegans (I like to rub miso over the vegetables to add lots of flavour.)
Sauce: use a peppercorn or bearnaise sauce

Couscous, Sweet Potato & Pomegranate Salad

There is something so hearty about the combination of couscous and sweet potato: it works for all seasons, whether you're wanting something warming in the winter or a side salad for a summer barbecue. Throw in some pomegranate and seeds and you have a salad that offers juicy crunches and mellow, cosy carbs in every bite!

1 large sweet potato (or 2 small), cut into small chunks (I leave the skin on, but remove any hard knobbly bits)
1 tbsp olive oil
sprinkle of paprika
60g (2¼oz) rocket (arugula)
2 spring onions (scallions), trimmed and diced
4 tbsp pomegranate seeds
2 tbsp sunflower seeds
100g (3½oz) feta, crumbled
120g (4¼oz) dried couscous, prepared according to packet instructions
salt and pepper

FOR THE DRESSING
4 tbsp olive oil
1 tsp lime juice
2 tsp honey
1–2 tbsp finely chopped fresh coriander (cilantro)

EQUIPMENT
chopping board—knife—baking tray
salad bowl—whisk or fork—salad tongs or two spoons

PREHEAT THE OVEN AND BAKE THE SWEET POTATO
Preheat the oven to 200°C (180°C fan/400°F/gas mark 6). Spread the sweet potato chunks out on the baking tray, drizzle with the olive oil and season with the paprika and some salt and pepper. Mix so each chunk is coated in oil and seasoning, then roast in the oven for 20 minutes.

MAKE THE DRESSING
While the sweet potato is in the oven, put the dressing ingredients in the salad bowl and season with salt and pepper. Mix well with a whisk or a fork until you have a smooth emulsified liquid (you can make the dressing in a separate bowl if you like, but I can never be bothered!).

THROW EVERYTHING IN THE DRESSING
Add the rocket, spring onions, pomegranate seeds, sunflower seeds, feta, couscous and sweet potato to the bowl of dressing and toss everything together with two spoons or salad tongs – you want every little piece of this salad to be kissed by the dressing!

SERVE
Serve and enjoy, it's that simple!

The salad will keep in the fridge in an airtight container for up to 3 days.

ALTERNATIVE INGREDIENTS
Couscous: use rice, bulgur wheat, quinoa or riced cauliflower
Sweet potato: use butternut squash, a normal potato, pumpkin (squash) or carrots
Sunflower seeds: use pumpkin seeds, sesame seeds, or your favourite packet of mixed seeds, or throw in some nuts instead – we are after that crunch, so raw veggies would work too if you can't eat nuts and seeds
Rocket (arugula): use chopped romaine (cos) or gem lettuce, or spinach
Feta: use goat's cheese, mozzarella or diced and roasted halloumi

Chicken &
Mushroom Pie

There's something so wholesome about a pie: hearty meats and veggies thrown into a thick gravy or creamy sauce and hugged in some pastry or mashed potato. For me, a puff pastry layer is an absolute must for this wintery sit-down dinner. A pie is like the language of love in British food culture – in typical British weather we often want to cuddle up with a pie and pint!

Make the chicken and mushroom filling up to a day before (or freeze it) and top with the pastry just before baking.

1 tbsp butter
500g (1lb 2oz) boneless, skinless chicken
    thighs, cut into bite-sized pieces
150g (5½oz) chestnut mushrooms, sliced
2 shallots, peeled and finely diced
1 tsp salt
1 tsp freshly ground black pepper
150g (5½oz) spinach
600ml (20fl oz/2½ cups) double (heavy)
    cream
1 tbsp wholegrain mustard
1 chicken stock (bouillon) pot dissolved
    in 200ml (7fl oz/generous ¾ cup)
    boiling water
50g (1¾oz) parmesan cheese, grated
1 x 320g (11¼oz) sheet of all-butter
    puff pastry

EQUIPMENT
chopping board—knife—grater—frying pan—wooden spoon—17 x 27cm (7 x 11in) ovenproof pie dish—large serving spoon

PREHEAT THE OVEN AND MAKE THE CHICKEN FILLING
Preheat the oven to 180°C (160°C fan/350°F/gas mark 4).
Melt the butter in the frying pan over a medium heat, add the chicken thighs and let them colour for 5 minutes, then add the mushrooms, shallots, salt and pepper and cook for 8 minutes until the mushrooms cook down and get slightly golden around the edges. Add the spinach, double cream, mustard, chicken stock and parmesan and simmer for 5–10 minutes until you have a thick gravy-like sauce coating the chicken.

ASSEMBLE AND BAKE THE PIE
Pour the pie filling into the pie dish and gently roll over the puff pastry, crimping it with the back of a fork (or your fingers) at the edge of the dish (make a pretty pattern on top with any leftover pastry if you like!). Bake in the oven for 15 minutes, until the pastry is golden brown.

SERVE
Remove the pie from the oven, get yourself a large serving spoon and crack into that flaky, hearty dinner!

Leftovers will keep in the fridge for 2–3 days, and the filling can be frozen for up to 3 months.

ALTERNATIVE INGREDIENTS
Chicken thighs: use chicken breasts or turkey breast
Double (heavy) cream: use single (light) cream or full-fat cream cheese
Mushrooms: use leeks or courgette (zucchini)
Spinach: use chopped chard or cavolo nero leaves
Puff pastry: use shortcrust (pie) or mashed potato
Make it veggie: remove the chicken and use a 400g (14oz) tin of butter beans, balancing out the weight of the chicken with vegetables. Use vegetable stock instead of chicken and add feta, more spinach or even ricotta to make the pie creamy and delicious.

Bolognese
Pasta Bake

Most Italians will probably tell me off for this one – please don't share it with your Nonna! 'Spag Bol', as it's called in our house, is a dish we pull out when we are all needing a hug. We usually cook a large batch of bolognese and freeze portions so when you need a big bowl of pasta with bolognese sauce, it's ready to go. This bake came about because I am a cheese monster: I top each layer of the bol with cheese as I eat it, then go in with another layer of cheese!

Make the beef mince ahead and freeze for up to 3 months.

generous drizzle of olive oil
2 red onions, peeled and finely diced
1 bulb of garlic, peeled and finely chopped
500g (1lb 2oz) minced (ground) beef
1 tsp dried oregano
1 tsp salt
1 tsp freshly ground black pepper
2 x 400g (14oz) tins chopped tomatoes
3 tbsp tomato purée (paste)
2 beef stock (bouillon) pots (don't need
    water, just add them as they are)
2 tbsp full-fat cream cheese
300g (10½oz) dried pasta of your choice,
    to serve
150g (5½oz) Cheddar cheese, grated
125g (4¼oz) mozzarella, grated

EQUIPMENT
chopping board—knife—grater—2 large,
deep saucepans—wooden spoon
20 x 28cm (8 x 11in) ovenproof dish—grater

MAKE THE BOLOGNESE
Heat the olive oil in a large, deep saucepan over a medium heat, throw in the onion and garlic, cook for a minute or two until softened then add the minced beef and cook until browned. Add the oregano, salt and pepper, chopped tomatoes, tomato purée, stock pots and cream cheese and cook for 20 minutes until the ragu is rich and thickened.

COOK THE PASTA
While that sauce is cooking, cook the pasta in another saucepan, in plenty of salted boiling water, for about 6 minutes until al dente.

PREHEAT THE OVEN AND ASSEMBLE AND BAKE THE DISH
Preheat the oven to 200°C (180°C fan/400°F/gas mark 6). Chuck the cooked pasta into the sauce and mix until fully coated. Transfer to the ovenproof dish and sprinkle the Cheddar cheese and mozzarella on top. Bake for 10 minutes (until your cheese is golden brown and bubbling).

SERVE
Serve up and enjoy this utterly delicious comfort food.

The sauce will keep in the fridge for up to 2 days.

ALTERNATIVE INGREDIENTS
Red onion: use white onions or shallots
Minced (ground) beef: use minced pork, lamb, vegan mince or 50% beef and 50% pork, or replace with 350g (12½oz) finely chopped mushrooms
Cream cheese: use double (heavy) cream or a vegan alternative
Beef stock (bouillon) pots: use vegetable stock
Oregano: use mixed dried herbs, Italian dried herbs or dried basil
Penne pasta: use any other shaped pasta you fancy
Mozzarella: use any other cheese that becomes stringy when melted

My Thermidor
Chips

We happened by a little pub on a walk in Cornwall. It was raining, we wanted a rest and craved beers and chips. We ordered 'Thermidor Chips' and they were so good that we returned every day for them (and for many more pints). They were ordinary chips with a creamy sauce, but they were just what you wanted when it's cold outside and you need warming through. Mum gave me the mission of recreating them. Somehow, I made them slightly better so I thought I would share my sacred recipe - Thermidor Chips, aka my seriously posh cheesy chips. Make the thermidor sauce up to 12 hours in advance, then warm it through before pouring it over the chips

600g (1lb 5oz) chips (chunky or fries will do)
50g (1¾oz) salted butter
2 shallots, peeled and finely diced
450ml (15fl oz/scant 2 cups) single (light) cream
a large handful of finely chopped fresh tarragon
180–200g (6½–7oz) parmesan cheese, grated
pinch of sea salt

EQUIPMENT
chopping board—knife—grater—baking tray to cook the chips on—large saucepan wooden spoon or whisk—serving bowl

GET THE CHIPS IN THE OVEN
Put the chips in the oven, cooking them according to the packet instructions.

MAKE THE SAUCE
While the chips are cooking, melt the butter in the large saucepan over a medium-low heat, then add the shallots and cook for 10 minutes or so, until super soft and sweet. Pour in the cream, add the tarragon and parmesan and stir or whisk, keeping it on a low heat until the parmesan melts and you have a gorgeously thick sauce. That's the sauce done.

FINAL TOUCHES
Pour the sauce over the chips, sprinkle with sea salt and serve.

Creamy
Garlic Chicken

SERVES 2

This recipe is basically a hug in a pan. Whatever cosy carb you are craving, this creamy garlic chicken is sure to satisfy whatever part of you that needs comforting! It's delicious mixed through pasta, or served on rice or mash. My favourite way to serve it is on mash with some green beans or peas. Put a cosy film on and you've got happy belly, happy Hari.

2 boneless, skinless chicken breasts
   (or 4 boneless, skinless thighs)
½ tsp salt
½ tsp freshly ground black pepper
½ tsp garlic granules
2 tbsp olive oil
2 tbsp salted butter
1 bulb of garlic, cloves peeled and finely
   chopped
2 shallots, peeled and finely diced
300ml (10fl oz/1¼ cups) chicken stock
   (bouillon)
150ml (5fl oz/⅔ cup) white wine
250ml (8fl oz/1 cup) single (light) cream
50g (1¾oz) parmesan cheese, grated
1 tbsp chopped parsley, to serve

EQUIPMENT
rolling pin—chopping board—knife—large
frying pan—wooden spoon—grater

START WITH THE CHICKEN
Bash the chicken breasts with a rolling pin until they're an even thickness, then season each side with the salt, pepper and garlic granules. Heat the olive oil in the frying pan over a medium-high heat, place the chicken in the pan and sear each side for 3–4 minutes, until golden brown. Remove them from the pan and set aside while you start making the sauce.

MAKE THAT CREAMY SAUCE
Throw the butter in the pan and add the garlic (yep, a whole bulb – trust me on this one) and shallots and cook over a medium heat for a few minutes until soft. Stir in the chicken stock, white wine and cream, bring to a simmer, then throw in the grated parmesan. Return the chicken breasts to the pan, cover with a lid (if you don't have a lid, a sheet of foil will do, if you don't have foil just add another 100ml/3½fl oz/scant ½ cup of chicken stock) and cook for 10 minutes until the sauce has thickened and the chicken is cooked through.

SERVE
When your sauce is thick and your chicken is cooked through, you're done. Spoon the chicken and sauce over your carb of choice, sprinkle over the parsley and that is it!

The dish will keep in the fridge for up to 2 days, and in the freezer for up to 3 months.

ALTERNATIVE INGREDIENTS
Chicken breasts: use turkey breast meat, or a meaty fish like a salmon, cod or halibut
Shallots: use onion, although the shallots just give a sweeter, less intense flavour
Chicken stock (bouillon): use vegetable stock
White wine: use more chicken stock
Single (light) cream: use double (heavy) cream or crème fraîche

Generations' Boxing Day Curried Parsnip Soup

SERVES 6

My nana passed this recipe down to my mum and it's been made every Boxing Day since I was born. It's a really simple soup but it's a crowd-pleaser. It's got warmth thanks to the curry powder and it takes next to no time to make. We enjoy ours with lots of tiger bread and butter after a long countryside walk to warm the cockles.

60g (2¼oz) butter
2 red onions, peeled and roughly diced
4 garlic cloves, peeled and finely chopped
500g (1lb 2oz) parsnips, peeled and diced
60g (2¼oz/½ cup) plain (all-purpose) flour
2 rounded tsp curry powder (choose your level of heat)
1 litre (34fl oz/2 pints) good-quality beef stock (bouillon)
150ml (5fl oz/⅔ cup) single (light) cream
salt and pepper

TO SERVE
a handful of finely chopped chives
olive oil, for drizzling

EQUIPMENT
chopping board—knife—deep, large saucepan with a lid—wooden spoon
stick blender or food processor

COOK THE VEGETABLES
Melt the butter in the large saucepan over a medium heat then add the onion, garlic and parsnips to the pan and fry gently for 5 minutes until everything has softened slightly. Stir in the flour and curry powder and cook for another minute then add the stock and season with salt and pepper. Bring to the boil, stir, cover with a lid and simmer for 15 minutes until the parsnips are tender.

BLEND THE SOUP
Let the soup cool for 5 minutes, then using a stick blender or a food processor, blend until smooth. Stir in the cream just before serving and taste to check the seasoning. Sprinkle the chives on top, add a drizzle of olive oil and enjoy.

The soup will keep in the fridge for 2–3 days, and in the freezer for up to 3 months.

COMFORT

in 40

Pulled Chicken Tacos

I make this whenever we have family over: it works for all the generations – my sister and I in our 20s, my cousins in their 30s, our parents in their 50–60s. Even Nana and Gramps who are in their mid 80s and have never had tacos before ate about 7 between them at our last family gathering! They are flavourful, you can forget about them as they cook and you can tailor them according to what the family loves (for example, I add a mega ton of cheese, avocado, soured cream and jalapeños).

3 tbsp olive oil
6 boneless chicken thighs
2 onions, peeled and diced
6–8 garlic cloves, peeled and finely
    chopped
1½ tsp ground cumin
1½ tsp ground coriander
1 tsp paprika
1½ tsp garlic granules
a pinch of dried chilli flakes (optional)
400g (14oz) tin tomatoes (or a tube of
    tomato purée/paste)
750ml (25fl oz/3 cups) chicken stock
    (bouillon)
8 mini tortilla wraps
fillings of choice (I use grated mozzarella
    cheese, jalapeños from a jar and a
    sprinkle of chopped coriander (cilantro))
salt and pepper
lime wedges, to serve

EQUIPMENT
chopping board—knife—large deep frying pan with a lid (for making taco filling) wooden spoon—shallow frying pan

COOK THE CHICKEN
Heat the oil in a large deep frying pan over a high heat, add the chicken thighs and sear on both sides until crispy (around 3–5 mins), then remove from the pan and set aside. In the same pan add the diced onions and garlic and cook for 5 minutes until soft, then add the spices and cook for 2 minutes before adding the tomatoes. Cook for 2 more minutes. Put the chicken back in the pan, season with salt and pepper and add the chicken stock (you need enough to cover the thighs), pop a lid on and cook for 30 minutes until the chicken can be pulled apart.

MAKE THE TACOS
Remove the pulled chicken from the pan, leaving the sauce. Add a tortilla wrap to the sauce and coat on both sides then add to a shallow frying pan over a medium heat and add your pulled chicken along with your chosen toppings, then fold the wrap over itself to make a taco. Let it cook for 1 minute on each side until crisp and golden brown, then remove it from the pan, garnish with coriander and fresh lime and enjoyyyyy. Repeat with the remaining tortillas and filling. If you have any sauce leftover, use it for dipping.

ALTERNATIVE INGREDIENTS
Chicken: I use thighs because they're juicier than breasts and don't dry out, but you could use lamb or beef. I have done this before with stewing beef and beef brisket and they're both real winners. Remember that beef and lamb require a longer cooking time before they will fall apart.
Chicken stock: use the same stock as meat that you're cooking. If you're cooking beef use beef stock.
Fillings: use grated cheese, cucumber, shredded lettuce, tomato, jalapeños, cooked rice, beans... the list is endless. Be creative and make it as fun as possible.

My Famous
Beef Ragu

SERVES 4-6

I shared this recipe with some followers one freezing-cold week in the winter of 2023. It's something I made when I worked in France during ski season. Guests would arrive on a Tuesday night and after a day of travelling and acclimatising to the cold temperatures of the Avoriaz ski slopes, this dish would warm them all up and get them excited about the next day's snow. It can be cooked on the hob, in the slow cooker, or in the Aga (the longer you cook it, the richer it gets but it can also be made in under forty minutes if you're in a hurry).

750g–1kg (1lb 10oz–2lb 4oz) stewing or braising beef, diced
1 tsp salt
1 tsp freshly ground black pepper
3–4 tbsp olive oil
2 red onions, peeled and thinly sliced
8 garlic cloves, peeled and finely chopped
3–4 carrots, peeled and finely diced
2 x 400g (14oz) tins chopped tomatoes
3 tbsp tomato purée (paste)
70g (2½oz) cooked unsmoked streaky bacon, finely chopped
150ml (5fl oz/⅔ cup) red wine
2–3 thyme sprigs
2–3 rosemary sprigs
2 beef stock (bouillon) cubes
pappardelle pasta, to serve

EQUIPMENT
chopping board—knife—large saucepan or casserole dish with a lid—wooden spoon

SEAR THE BEEF AND MAKE THE BASE
Season the beef with the salt and pepper. Heat the oil in the large saucepan over a medium-high heat, then sear the meat for a few minutes until browned. Work in batches so that it sears instead of simmering. Remove it from the pan and set aside. Add the onion and garlic to the pan and cook for a few minutes until softened, then add the carrots and cook for a few minutes longer before adding the tomatoes, purée, bacon, wine, thyme and rosemary. Crumble the stock cubes into the pan and then add the seared beef and all its resting juices.

SIT BACK AND LET THE MAGIC HAPPEN
Stir, pop the lid on and cook the ragu low and slow for as long as you've got (the tastiest for me is leaving it for 2–4 hours and forgetting about it), stirring occasionally, but if you only have 40 minutes it's still going to be delicious.

SERVE
Mix the ragu through the pappardelle pasta so that it is coated in the thick sauce and then serve.

The ragu will keep in the fridge for 2–3 days, and in the freezer for up to 3 months.

ALTERNATIVE INGREDIENTS
Beef: to make this veggie or vegan use 160–200g dried porcini mushrooms, rehydrated before you use them, or chopped sweet potato
Bacon: the bacon can be taken out completely, I mainly add it for a meaty salty taste. It can be substituted with 2 chopped anchovies
Red wine: use an extra 150ml (5fl oz/⅔ cup) beef stock (bouillon)

Cheesy Fish Pie

One of the reasons comfort food means so much to me is because it is so simple: you throw a few ingredients together, whack them in the oven and then you have something that can be shared with loved ones. This fish pie is just that. We had it on rainy winter evenings when we got in from school: it was creamy, cheesy, with chunks of our favourite fish in it. Whether you make it for a dinner party or a family night, there will be smiles all around.

1kg (2lb 4oz) potatoes (I like to use russet potatoes), peeled and cut into chunks
25g (1oz) salted butter
glug of whole (full-fat) milk
70g (2½oz) extra mature (super sharp) Cheddar cheese, grated
lots of crushed black pepper

FOR THE FILLING
25g (1oz) butter
1 white onion, peeled and finely diced
6 garlic cloves, peeled and finely chopped
2 tbsp plain (all-purpose) flour (or cornflour/cornstarch)
500ml (17fl oz/generous 2 cups) whole (full-fat) milk
70g (2½oz) mature (sharp) Cheddar cheese, grated
600g (1lb 5oz) boneless, skinless fish of choice, cut into bite-sized chunks
60g (2¼oz) garden peas

EQUIPMENT
peeler—chopping board—knife—grater
large saucepan—colander—masher
medium frying pan—26 x 30cm (10 x 12in)
ovenproof dish

PREHEAT THE OVEN AND PREPARE THE MASH
Preheat the oven to 180°C (160°C fan/350°F/gas mark 4). Put the potato chunks in a large saucepan, cover with salted cold water and bring to the boil. Cook for 20 minutes or so until soft and mashable. Strain and return to the pan then throw in the butter, the glug of milk, cheese and pepper and mash until smooth.

MAKE THE FISH PIE FILLING
While your potatoes are cooking, make the fish pie filling. Melt the butter in the frying pan over a medium heat, add the onion and garlic and cook for 5 minutes until soft. Sprinkle over the flour and stir for 10 seconds until a paste begins to form, then pour in the milk little by little, stirring constantly, until the sauce thickens (keep mixing as you add the milk, to avoid any lumps). Remove the sauce from the heat and throw in most of the grated cheese – the residual heat will melt it and it will continue to melt when it's in the oven.

BAKE AND SERVE
Mix the fish and peas into the sauce, then pour it into the ovenproof dish. Dollop the mashed potato over the top and spread out with the back of a fork. I like to drag the fork along the mash so those top bits go extra crispy in the oven. Sprinkle the remaining cheese on top and bung it in the oven for 10 minutes until the sides are bubbling and the top is golden!

The pie can be frozen before it's baked for 1–2 months (and cooked from frozen, although add another 5–10 minutes to the cooking time). After baking, the pie will keep in the fridge for up to 2 days.

ALTERNATIVE INGREDIENTS
Potatoes: use sweet potatoes, puff or a shortcrust (pie) pastry instead
Fish: use a couple of bags of frozen mixed fish, or any fish you fancy. Meaty fish and shellfish such as cod, haddock, salmon, hake, halibut, tuna, shelled prawns (shrimp) and monkfish work best in this dish. Mix up the ratios as you wish - you just need 600g (1lb 5oz) of it.

Minty Lamb Chops
& Rustic New Potatoes

I was once invited to a farm to show my followers how eating from the land can be super easy, and with a few ingredients that we sourced from their livestock, vegetable and herb garden we made a delicious dinner. Something special about this recipe is that the seasoning that you use to cook the meat, you use to flavour the potatoes, so you don't need lots of ingredients, just a few good-quality ones.

1kg (2lb 4oz) new potatoes, halved
25g (1oz) salted butter
1 tbsp finely chopped fresh mint
1 tbsp finely chopped fresh rosemary
good pinch of salt
8 locally-sourced lamb chops (they'll be more flavourful from your local butcher)
4 tbsp olive oil
1 bulb of garlic, skin-on cloves bashed with the flat side of a knife blade

EQUIPMENT
chopping board—knife—saucepan
strainer/colander—wooden spoon
griddle pan

START WITH THE SPUDS
Put the halved new potatoes in the saucepan, cover with salted cold water, bring to the boil and cook for about 15 minutes (you want them just over part-boiled, so they're almost soft - I find this way the butter and flavours really soak into the potatoes rather than just coat the outside). Strain and give them a shake so each one is a little bashed up (this is how the flavours soak in). While they're still hot add 20g (¾oz) of the salted butter, half the finely chopped herbs and all the salt. Mix until the potatoes are coated in the herbs, butter and salt.

PREP THE LAMB CHOPS
While your potatoes are cooking, or once they're done, rub the lamb chops in olive oil, the other half of the fresh herbs and salt to taste.

GET THEM SIZZLING
Heat a griddle pan over a medium-high heat until hot, then lay the lamb chops in the pan and cook them for about 3 minutes on each side. When you've cooked one side, flip the lamb chops and chuck the rest of the butter into the pan along with all the garlic cloves. When this garlic butter is running around the pan, tilt the pan and spoon it over each of the chops to baste them in these flavours.

REST AND SERVE
After about 6 minutes your lamb chops should be pink (if you want them more well done, cook for an extra minute on each side). Remove from the pan and let them rest.

Serve up your potatoes and pop your lamb chops on top. I like to add an extra pinch of salt and a dollop of mint sauce and there you have a beautifully flavoured dinner.

Butter Chicken
Curry Pie

Many of us will be familiar with butter chicken, the curry that melts in your mouth, is packed with flavour and is often made when someone needs a cuddle. Here, I have made it into a pie so when you crack through that puff pastry top you still have your treasure trove of comfort food beneath. Don't be alarmed by the ingredients list: once the spices are in your cupboard they last for ages and – trust me – you're going to be making this over and over again.

500g (1lb 2oz) block of puff pastry

FOR THE CHICKEN
1kg (2lb 4oz) boneless and skinless
   chicken thighs, diced
8 tbsp full-fat Greek yoghurt
1 tbsp lemon juice
1 tsp salt
6 garlic cloves, peeled and finely chopped
1 tbsp finely chopped ginger
1 tsp garam masala
1 red chilli, chopped
½ tsp ground turmeric

MARINATE THE CHICKEN
Put the chicken in a large bowl and add the yoghurt, lemon juice, salt, garlic, ginger and spices for the marinade. Mix to coat and leave in the fridge for a couple of hours if you can (don't stress if you can't – it won't affect the dish that much).

FRY THE CHICKEN
Once the chicken has marinated, add a tablespoon of butter to a frying pan over a medium-low heat, add the chicken and fry until coloured (it doesn't have to be cooked through, you just want the outside to have some colour). Remove from the pan and set aside (you can pop it back in the bowl you used with the marinade).

PREHEAT THE OVEN AND MAKE THE SAUCE
Preheat the oven to 200°C (180°C fan/400°F/gas mark 6). Add the rest of the butter to the pan you fried the chicken in and add the caraway seeds, star anise, cinnamon stick and cloves. Cook over a medium-high heat until the caraway seeds start to fizz, then add the onion and cook for 5–6 minutes until soft. Add the garlic and ginger and cook for a minute – it will start smelling delicious – then add all the remaining spices along with the tomato purée. Stir for a few minutes then turn down the heat. Add the chopped tomatoes and chicken and cook for 10 minutes, then add the cream and cook for another 5 minutes (some people remove the chicken and blend the sauce at this stage, but I like the texture and don't think this is necessary).

recipe continued

FOR THE SAUCE

4 tbsp butter

1 tsp caraway seeds

1 star anise

1 cinnamon stick

4 cloves

1 large white onion, peeled and sliced
   or diced

8 garlic cloves, peeled and finely chopped

1 tbsp finely chopped ginger

2 tsp ground cumin

2 tsp garam masala

2 tsp ground coriander

2 tbsp tomato purée (paste)

2 x 400g (14oz) tins chopped tomatoes

350ml (12fl oz/1½ cups) double
   (heavy) cream

1 tsp salt

EQUIPMENT

chopping board—knife—large bowl
spoon—frying pan—wooden spoon
pie dish—rolling pin

ASSEMBLE AND BAKE

Pop the chicken curry into a pie dish then cover with the rolled out puff pastry. Poke a few tiny holes in the pastry to allow steam to escape and crimp the edges. Pop it in the oven for about 20 minutes until the pastry is golden brown (brush it with beaten egg beforehand if you like, but shop-bought pastry doesn't necessarily need it).

SERVE

Take it out the oven and spoon into that treasure trove of flavour – serve and enjoy.

ALTERNATIVE INGREDIENTS

For this recipe you don't really want to be substituting ingredients because it is such a delicious dinner. Once you get these spices in your cupboard, you'll be making it over and over again!

Dirty Chicken
& Waffles (ish)

MAKES 6 PIECES OF
CHICKEN

When I was at university in Oxford there was a restaurant that served the best fried chicken and waffles. I had never had this combination before but once I tried it I understood why it worked so well: the sweet waffles with maple syrup and the salty, crispy chicken made for a flavour fountain that I couldn't turn off. I went home and tried to recreate it, using shop-bought waffles (who has a waffle maker at uni?!), covering the chicken in buttermilk and coming up with this delicious dish! This is the perfect recipe for a brunch, lunch or dinner and surprise guests with something they probably haven't tried before.

about 500ml (17fl oz/generous 2 cups)
    sunflower or vegetable oil, for frying
6 boneless, skinless chicken thighs

FOR THE COATING
400ml (14fl oz/1¾ cups) buttermilk
1 tsp salt
1 tsp ground black pepper
1 tsp garlic granules
1 tsp paprika

FOR THE CRISPY CRUST
400g (14oz/3 cups) plain (all-purpose)
    flour
1 tsp baking powder
2 tsp garlic granules
1 tsp paprika
1 tsp salt
1 tsp ground black pepper

HEAT THE OIL
Pour the oil into the saucepan, place over a medium-low heat and let it heat up slowly, being careful to not let it get too hot: you want it to fizz when you add the chicken, not get so hot that it boils and spits. Please be careful here!

COAT THE CHICKEN
Combine the buttermilk, salt, pepper, garlic granules and paprika in a bowl and mix well.

Put the flour, baking powder, garlic granules, paprika, salt and pepper in a separate bowl and mix well so the spices are evenly distributed.

Dunk the chicken thighs one by one in the marinade, letting the excess drip off, then coat them in the flour mix and pop to one side on a plate. Some of the flour will soak into the buttermilk, so when all the thighs are coated, repeat the process to give them an extra thick and crispy layer of crust on the outside.

TIME TO FRY THOSE THIGHS!
When all the chicken has been double dunked, it's time to fry it. Test the temperature of the oil by dunking a little bit of the chicken into the oil: if the oil starts to fizz around the chicken it's ready, if nothing happens it needs a little longer to warm up, and if it starts to bubble, take the chicken out and reduce the temperature (cooling oil takes a while, so it may take 10 minutes for it to reach the right temperature). Fry the chicken in the oil for 4 minutes on one side and 4 minutes on the other (cook 3 thighs at a time), turning the thighs with tongs. Carefully remove the chicken from the oil and lay on some kitchen paper on a plate to absorb excess oil. If you think your chicken needs cooking a little more, but it's already golden, you can pop it in the oven for 5 minutes just to ensure it's cooked all the way through.

recipe continued

TO SERVE
Belgian sugar waffles
maple syrup, for drizzling

EQUIPMENT
saucepan—2 bowls—plate for raw meat
plate for cooked meat—metal tongs

SERVE
Toast your waffles if you like then top with the fried chicken and drizzle over some maple syrup.

ALTERNATIVE INGREDIENTS
Chicken thighs: use chicken breasts or chicken thighs with bone intact (I just find it gets fiddly when you're cutting into it)
Seasoning: this is another recipe where the seasoning is relative to you, I use these flavours because I don't want too much going on, I want to taste the sweet and saltiness but if there is a spice that you love, why not try it here. In particular, oregano, onion salt, garlic salt, cayenne pepper and parsley all work well.

Lamb & Butter Bean
Stew with Feta & Mint

This easy, hearty stew warms the soul. For me, lamb and feta work beautifully together. This recipe is too simple not to make: you just throw everything in one dish, leave it in the oven or on the stove to make the house smell divine, and are left with a scrummy dinner! When the weather is closing in and you want something comforting in the oven, this stew, served with a crunchy French baguette for dunking, is what dreams are made of.

knob of butter
1 red onion, peeled and finely diced
1 bulb of garlic, cloves peeled and
   finely chopped
400g (14oz) tin chopped tomatoes
1 tsp salt
1 tsp ground black pepper
800g (1lb 12oz) lamb shoulder, cut into
   bite-sized chunks
200ml (7fl oz/generous ¾ cup) red wine
650ml (22fl oz/2¾ cups) lamb stock (made
   with 2 lamb stock/bouillon cubes)
sprig of rosemary
2 x 400g (14oz) tins butter beans
   (lima beans)

TO SERVE
a few sprigs of fresh mint, leaves chopped
150g (5½oz) feta
1 large French baguette

EQUIPMENT
chopping board—knife—large casserole
dish with a lid—wooden spoon

GET THE STEW GOING

Melt the butter in the casserole dish over a medium heat, throw in the onion and garlic (I know a whole bulb sounds like a lot, but it mellows out through the cooking process and just gives the dish a lovely hum) and cook for 2 minutes until soft then add the tomatoes, salt, pepper, lamb chunks, red wine, lamb stock and the sprig of rosemary. Cover with a lid and either pop it in the oven at 200°C (180°C fan/400°F/gas mark 6) for 30 minutes or cook it on the hob (stirring from time to time if your dish isn't non-stick).

ADD THE BUTTER BEANS

After 30 minutes, add the butter beans and cook for 10 minutes longer. Remove the rosemary sprig.

SERVE

Serve the fragrant stew with the feta crumbled on top and a sprinkling of chopped mint. I have mine with sliced French baguette slathered with salted butter.

The stew will keep in the fridge for up to 3 days, and in the freezer for up to 3 months.

ALTERNATIVE INGREDIENTS

Lamb: use beef (stewing beef is fine but increase the cooking time). To make it vegan use a meat alternative or a hearty vegetable like sweet potato, swede or mushrooms (such as portobello)
Butter: use olive oil
Red wine: use more stock
Lamb stock (bouillon): use chicken or beef stock, or vegetable stock if making it veggie/vegan
Feta: use a goat's cheese, parmesan or a dollop of ricotta, or dairy-free alternative

'Man Flu' Chicken Soup

Drizzly and miserable weather calls for my 'Man Flu' Chicken Soup. It's the ideal way to use up a chicken carcass after a roast dinner, though you can of course roast a chicken purely for this soup and make a bigger batch – it freezes perfectly, and you can add the roasting juices to the soup too.

chicken cooking juices (keep those juices, if available) (optional)
2 red onions, peeled and finely diced
4 carrots, peeled and cut into 1–2cm (½–¾in) pieces
3 leeks, trimmed and cut into 1–2cm (½–¾in) pieces
1 bulb of garlic, cloves peeled and finely chopped
300–400g (10½–14oz) shredded cooked chicken (I like to use super-juicy chicken thighs)
1-2 tsp freshly chopped herbs (rosemary/sage/thyme)
1 tsp salt
1 tsp freshly ground black pepper
1 litre (34fl oz/2 pints) chicken stock (bouillon)
100g (3½oz) peas
bread and butter, to serve

EQUIPMENT
chopping board—knife—large heavy-based saucepan—wooden spoon

COOK THE VEGETABLES
If you have any chicken cooking juices, put them in the large saucepan. Add the diced onion, carrots, leeks and garlic and cook over a medium heat for about 20 minutes, until everything is soft and almost falling apart on its own.

ADD THE STOCK AND SIMMER
Add the chicken, the sprigs of thyme, salt and pepper. Add the chicken stock, cover and simmer for about 10 minutes, to allow the flavours to infuse and ensure those vegetables are super soft and succulent. (I never like hard vegetables when I am feeling rubbish. I always want them to be soft in a soup.) Add the peas and simmer for 2 more minutes.

BLEND (OPTIONAL) THEN SERVE
Blend the soup if you want, however I love to leave it so it's almost like a chicken broth. Serve in a bowl with a hearty portion of bread and butter.

The soup will keep in the fridge for 2–3 days, and in the freezer for up to 3 months.

ALTERNATIVE INGREDIENTS
Chicken: use any leftover roast dinner meat, or for a veggie or vegan soup, use extra-firm tofu cut into bite-size pieces, and add it at the same time as the vegetables
Vegetables: use any vegetables – a favourite of mine is finely chopped chestnut mushrooms which can be added with the other vegetables
For extra oomph: add chopped potato or bulgur wheat (at the same time as the other vegetables) or else add your favourite noodles during the final 5 minutes cooking time

Dragon Pie 'with Dragons Caught from the Welsh Mountains'

My mum drives all over England for work and on the days she went to Wales (where she was born) she would tell us that she had caught some dragons in the Welsh mountains and was going to make a pie for dinner. We would be slightly traumatised yet excited at the same time at the prospect of having dragon for dinner...
It took us a lot longer than I care to admit to realise that she was using beef instead!

50g (1¾oz) butter
1 large red onion, peeled and finely diced
6–8 garlic cloves, peeled and finely chopped
1 tsp finely chopped fresh ginger
1 red chilli, finely chopped (deseed for less heat)
450–500g (1lb–1lb 2oz) diced short rib or stirloin steak
2 tbsp cornflour (cornstarch)
1–2 tsp Worcestershire sauce
300ml (10fl oz/1¼ cups) Guinness
300ml (10fl oz/1¼ cups) water
2 beef stock (bouillon) pots
1 x 320g (11¼oz) sheet of all-butter puff pastry
mashed potato, to serve
green beans, to serve

EQUIPMENT
chopping board—knife—deep, large saucepan with lid—wooden spoon
26cm (10in) pie dish

BROWN THE BEEF
Melt the butter in the large saucepan over a medium heat, throw in the onion, garlic, ginger and chilli and cook for 5 minutes until softened. Add the diced beef and let it brown for another 5 minutes, then sprinkle in the cornflour and stir to coat.

SIMMER, SIMMER
Add the Worcestershire sauce, Guinness, water and beef stock pots. Stir, cover with the lid and simmer for 15–20 minutes until the sauce has thickened.

PREHEAT THE OVEN, ASSEMBLE THE PIE AND BAKE
Preheat the oven to 220°C (fan 200°C/425°F/gas mark 7). Add the beef to the pie dish, roll out the puff pastry on top and crimp it at the edges of your pie dish with the back of a fork or your fingers. Bake in the oven for 10 minutes until the pastry is golden brown. Serve with mashed potato and boiled green beans and enjoy this fiery beef pie!

The beef filling will keep in the fridge for 2–3 days, and in the freezer for up to 3 months.

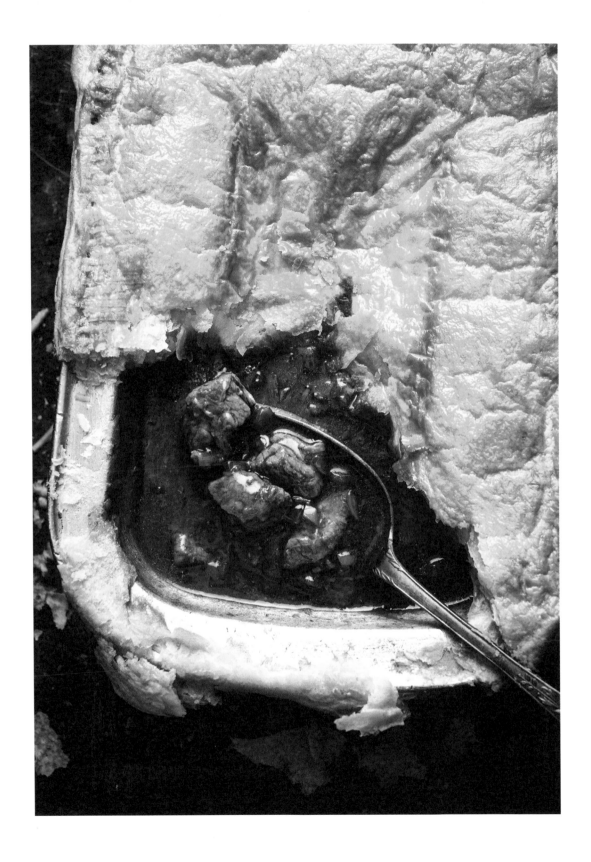

Wellies Off, Traybake in (Sticky, Chicken & Chorizo Style)

SERVES 6

Comfort food means home and family to me, and this versatile recipe is one that we loved to make after school because you can shove it in the oven and the whole family adores it. It's salty, sticky and the family highlight of the evening (it's also really good to make as a big batch for meal prep throughout the week). You can literally throw anything in this and mix it up – it's a great way to use up leftovers and vegetables in the fridge. I like to use chicken thighs with the skin on and let them get super crispy in the oven.

1kg (2lb 4oz) new potatoes, diced
800g (1lb 12oz) cherry tomatoes
400g (14oz) tin butter (lima) beans, drained
3 red (bell) peppers, deseeded and
   roughly chopped
2 red onions, peeled and sliced
1 bulb of garlic, cloves peeled and
   finely chopped
2 tsp dried thyme (or a few sprigs of fresh)
1 tsp freshly ground black pepper
200g (7oz) Spanish chorizo sausage,
   cut into small pieces
8 chicken thighs (skin on or off, boneless
   or not, it's up to you)
500ml (17fl oz/generous 2 cups)
   chicken stock (bouillon)
2 tbsp honey
salt
parsley, to serve (optional)
feta, to serve (optional)

EQUIPMENT
chopping board—knife—large roasting tray

Preheat your oven to 200°C (180°C fan/400°F/gas mark 6).

CHUCK EVERYTHING IN THE TRAY
Throw the potatoes into a large roasting tray, along with the tomatoes, butter beans, peppers and onions. Sprinkle the garlic over everything, add the thyme, pepper and season with salt to taste. Mix everything together so it's all coated in the seasoning. Throw in the chorizo and place the chicken thighs on top.

ADD THE CHICKEN STOCK AND BAKE
Pour over the chicken stock and season the top of each thigh with a little salt and any other herbs and spices you fancy, then drizzle the honey over everything. Bake in the oven for 40 minutes (time to shower, get your PJs on and have a little you time). If you find that the top of anything is catching, just pop a sheet of foil over the tray. Remove from the oven and serve with the fresh parsley scattered over the top, if using. I also love to crumble feta on the top for extra saltiness and flavour.

ALTERNATIVE INGREDIENTS
Cherry tomatoes and (bell) peppers: use carrots, courgette (zucchini), asparagus, green beans or broccoli
Honey: use maple or golden syrup, or a little sprinkle of brown sugar
Thyme: use basil, oregano or rosemary (I love throwing some paprika into this too)

Beer-battered Fish Sandwich

In Britain, Fish and Chip Fridays are a must, especially when winter draws in and all you want to do is sit with a sheet of newspaper in your lap that is almost burning the top of your legs from those salt and vinegar chips that are sat upon them. In the summer, however, you don't always want the heaviness of the meal but you might still crave crispy beer-battered fish, and that's how this beer-battered fish sandwich came about. It's a whopper!

1 litre (34fl oz/2 pints) vegetable oil, for frying
2 x 150g (5½oz) skinless, boneless pieces of cod
2 tbsp plain (all-purpose) flour
1 tsp salt
115g (4oz) ciabatta roll, halved
2 generous tbsp tartare sauce
romaine (cos) lettuce leaves, shredded
2 pickles or gherkins, sliced
1 lemon, halved

FOR THE BEER BATTER
50g (1¾oz/generous ⅓ cup) plain (all-purpose) flour
50g (1¾oz/generous ⅓ cup) cornflour (cornstarch)
1 tsp baking powder
1 tsp salt
1 tsp ground black pepper
1 tbsp white wine vinegar
100ml (3½fl oz/scant ½ cup) lager beer

EQUIPMENT
chopping board—knife—large deep saucepan—2 bowls—whisk—metal tongs plate lined with kitchen paper

HEAT THE OIL
Pour the oil into the large saucepan, place over a medium-low heat and let it heat up slowly (so you have more control over the heat – if it gets too hot too quickly it could bubble and boil, which is dangerous because it can spit and burn you – we are just after a little fizz!)

MAKE THE BEER BATTER
Mix the flour, cornflour, baking powder, salt and pepper in a bowl then add the vinegar and slowly pour in the lager, whisking as you do, until you have a smooth batter (similar to a pancake batter).

NOW WE ARE COOKING WITH OIL
Mix the flour and salt together in a small bowl, then dunk a piece of fish in the seasoned flour before adding it to the batter. Coat it fully then using the tongs, transfer to the hot oil... please, please be careful here: dunk a small part of the fish in first and if it fizzes it's perfect so pop the rest in. Repeat with the other piece of fish and cook for 2–3 minutes on each side until golden brown and crispy! Transfer to a plate lined with kitchen paper, to absorb the excess oil.

ASSEMBLE YOUR SANDWICHES
Toast the ciabatta, spread a generous dollop of tartare sauce over one half of each piece of ciabatta, add some crispy romaine lettuce and sliced gherkins, layer on your crispy battered fish, season with a good pinch of sea salt, serve with the lemon halves and enjoy!

ALTERNATIVE INGREDIENTS
Cod: use any other meaty white fish such as haddock or halibut
Fillings: my partner throws mushy peas and ketchup in his, my mum opts for mayo and throws oven-cooked chips in her ciabatta... it really is your choice!

Leftover Roast Dinner Hot-pot

SERVES 4

If you're anything like my family, you probably have some leftover meat in the fridge at the end of the weekend, maybe from roast chicken, pork, lamb or beef. This wholesome hot-pot is a great way to use leftovers. It's so simple: most of the ingredients are storecupboard staples, or vegetables you're likely to have hanging around. It's perfect for a cosy night in.

2 tbsp olive oil
1 red onion, peeled and diced
6 garlic cloves, peeled and finely chopped
1 tbsp garlic granules
1 tsp dried thyme
large pinch each of salt and pepper
400g (14oz) tin chopped tomatoes
400g (14oz) tin cannellini beans, drained and rinsed
about 400g (14oz) leftover cooked meat (leg of lamb in this is beautiful), roughly chopped
400g (14oz) potatoes, thinly sliced (peeled or not, it's up to you)

EQUIPMENT
chopping board—knife—deep frying pan
wooden spoon—ovenproof serving dish
(such as a lasagne dish)—large bowl

PREHEAT THE OVEN AND MAKE THE FILLING
Preheat the oven to 200°C (180°C fan/400°F/gas mark 6). Heat the oil in the frying pan over a medium heat, add the onion and garlic and cook for a few minutes until softened (if you're using raw meat, pop it in now and cook until the meat is seared). If you're using leftover cooked meat, just wait a minute. Add the garlic granules, thyme, salt and pepper, then throw in the chopped tomatoes and cannellini beans and the leftover cooked meat. Stir and transfer to the ovenproof dish.

PREP THE POTATOES AND BAKE THE HOT-POT
Put the slices of potato in a large bowl and add a drizzle of olive oil, salt, pepper and garlic granules. Mix to coat, then lay the slices on top of the meat in the dish. Bake in the oven for 20–25 minutes, until the potato is cooked and golden brown and the edges are of the hot-pot are bubbling.

SERVE
Remove from the oven, serve and enjoy.

The hot pot will keep in the fridge in an airtight container for 2 days, or up to 1 month in the freezer.

ALTERNATIVE INGREDIENTS
Red onion: use white onion or shallots
Chopped tomatoes: use 2 tbsp tomato purée (paste) and 200ml (7fl oz/ generous ¾ cup) good-quality meat stock (bouillon)
Cannellini beans: use butter (lima) beans, red kidney beans or mixed beans
Potato: use sweet potato if you're looking for a slightly healthier option

Moroccan Chicken Dinner
with Tahini Yoghurt

SERVES 4

This chicken dinner is great for any time of year, which is probably why I have such an attachment to it, and it's packed with flavour which means the taste buds will be tingling and it will be a recipe you make for a lifetime! It's perfect served warm or left to cool for serving at a barbecue or for a lunch made in advance.

4 chicken breasts
300g (10½oz) couscous
juice of 1 lemon
60–70g (2¼–2½oz) fresh rocket (arugula)
4 red (bell) peppers, deseeded and cut into bite-sized pieces
salt and pepper

FOR THE MARINADE
4 tbsp olive oil
1 tsp ground cumin
4 garlic cloves, peeled and finely chopped
1 tsp ground coriander
½ tsp ground turmeric

FOR THE TAHINI YOGHURT
4 tbsp tahini
4 tbsp full-fat Greek yoghurt

TO SERVE
150g (5½oz) pomegranate seeds
80g (2¾oz) feta, crumbled

EQUIPMENT
chopping board—knife—2 large bowls
spoon—baking tray—frying pan—small
bowl

PREHEAT THE OVEN AND MARINATE THE CHICKEN
Preheat the oven to 200°C (180°C fan/400°F/gas mark 6). Put the olive oil, cumin, garlic, coriander, turmeric, a tablespoon of salt and pepper in the large bowl. Add the chicken breasts, mix to coat and pop to one side for 10 minutes while you prepare the couscous.

PREPARE THE COUSCOUS
Cook the couscous according to the packet instructions then fluff it up, squeeze over the lemon juice and mix in the rocket along with a pinch each of salt and pepper.

COOK THE CHICKEN AND CHAR THE PEPPERS
Pop the marinated chicken on a baking tray in the oven to cook for 25 minutes, or until cooked through. Meanwhile, place the frying pan over a medium-high heat and throw in the peppers. Let them char for a few minutes – you want them to have brown bits on the skin.

MAKE THE YOGHURT AND SERVE
Combine the tahini and the yoghurt in the small bowl. Plate the couscous along with your sliced chicken, a dollop of the tahini yoghurt, a sprinkle of pomegranate seeds and crumble of feta, serve and enjoy.

Any leftovers will keep in the fridge for up to 3 days. If reheating, reheat until piping hot.

ALTERNATIVE INGREDIENTS
(Bell) peppers: use any colour (red is the sweetest) or use tomatoes, courgette (zucchini) or sweet potato
Couscous: swap for quinoa or bulgur wheat
Tahini and Greek yoghurt: swap for 4 large dollops of hummus
Make it veggie or vegan: swap chicken for halloumi or another vegetarian alternative, or for a vegan version, swap chicken for tofu or sweet potato. Swap the Greek yoghurt for a Greek-style plant-based yoghurt alternative or hummus (and leave out the feta).

Family Night
Fajita Lasagne

SERVES 4

One of my favourite cuisines is Mexican: it's so flavourful and colourful, and often it involves bringing people together, whether that's round a plate of sizzling fajitas or a jug of margarita. It's food to be enjoyed and shared with everyone. That is how I came up with this fajita lasagne, my love for Italian and Mexican flavours combined (if you have Italian heritage, I am sorry if this crosses the line!).

2 tbsp olive oil
2 onions, peeled and finely sliced
3 skinless and boneless chicken breasts, cut into strips
2 (bell) peppers, deseeded and sliced
2 tsp paprika
2 tsp ground cumin
1 tsp dried oregano
1 tsp ground coriander
400g (14oz) tin red kidney beans, drained
400g (14oz) tin tomatoes
8–10 lasagne sheets
100g (3½oz) mature (sharp) Cheddar cheese, grated
sliced jalapeños from a jar
salt and pepper

FOR THE BÉCHAMEL SAUCE
50g (1¾oz) butter
1 tbsp plain (all purpose) flour
250g (9oz) cream cheese
100–200ml (3½–7fl oz/scant ½–1 cup) milk

EQUIPMENT
chopping board—knife—grater—frying pan—wooden spoon—saucepan—whisk
17 x 27cm (7 x 11in) baking dish

MAKE THE FILLING
Add the olive oil to the frying pan and place over a medium heat. Soften the onions, then add the chicken. When it's partly cooked, add the peppers and spices, season with salt and pepper and cook until the chicken is cooked through. Add the kidney beans and tinned tomatoes, mix and leave to simmer while you make the béchamel sauce.

MAKE THE BÉCHAMEL SAUCE
Melt the butter in a separate saucepan over a low heat, whisk in the flour and when it forms a paste add the cream cheese a little at a time until you get a thick mixture. Next, add the milk a little at a time, whisking continuously, until you get a lovely thick sauce (you may not need all of the milk).

LAYER EVERYTHING TOGETHER AND BAKE
Start with some of the chicken and pepper mixture, spreading a layer of it in the bottom of the baking dish, then add a layer of lasagne sheets and spread them with a thin layer of the béchamel. Add a layer of Cheddar and repeat this layering process until you have run out of ingredients. Finish with some jalapeños on top to give it a little kick. Pop it in the oven for 15 minutes until the cheese starts to bubble and turn golden brown and enjoy.

ALTERNATIVE INGREDIENTS
Chicken: use any meat you fancy. Turkey breast or beef strips would work well
Spices: use fajita seasoning sachets for ease if you don't have all the spices
Red kidney beans: use black beans or add refried beans to the layers to make it a little more Mexican
Cheese: use your favourite cheese. Mozzarella, Jarlsberg or Red Leicester all work well
Jalapeños: swerve the heat and add crushed tortilla crisps for a crispy finish instead

COMFORT IN 40 **163**

Chicken Chilli
con Carne

SERVES 4

I have always loved chilli con carne. Every member of my family has different ways of eating it, but it satisfies all of our comfort food needs: my sister and dad have it on French bread with butter lathered on, I like it with fluffy rice and cheese, and my mum is a jacket potato woman... we all have our cosy carb of choice. Using succulent chicken thighs changes things up, but keeps the simplicity of the regular everyday chilli con carne.

This recipe works well in a slow cooker: I enjoy it as a weekend lunch, throwing everything in the slow cooker in the morning, getting on with my day, then coming back to it a few hours later!

good drizzle of olive oil
1 red onion, peeled and diced
6 garlic cloves, peeled and chopped
6 boneless, skinless chicken thighs, cut
    into small bite-sized chunks or strips
2 tsp cumin
2 tsp coriander
2 tsp paprika
pinch of dried chilli flakes
300ml (10fl oz/1¼ cups) chicken stock
400g (14oz) tin of chopped tomatoes
2 tbsp tomato puree (paste)
400g (14oz) tin of kidney beans
1 tsp salt
1 tsp crushed black pepper

EQUIPMENT
chopping board—knife—large saucepan or
large deep frying pan—wooden spoon

COOK THE CHILLI

Heat the oil in a large saucepan or frying pan over a medium heat, add the onion and garlic and cook for a couple of minutes until soft, then throw in the chicken and cook until browned, then sprinkle in all the spices and continue to cook until the chicken is cooked through. Add the chicken stock, chopped tomatoes and tomato puree, stir, bring to a simmer, then add the kidney beans and simmer for 15 minutes until the sauce reduces slightly – when it gets to the consistency you want, you're ready to serve!

Dad's Proper Chilli

My parents' divorce was really tough for my sister and me. We really struggled with the separation and the whole 'two Christmasses, two birthdays' was quite frankly rubbish. But one positive thing that came out of my parents' divorce was the fact that Dad learnt to cook and he PERFECTED his chilli. The only 'good' thing about having to leave our family home and go to our dad's flat was the fact we were guaranteed to be served Dad's chilli. That is the definition of comfort food for me, and could possibly be where my love for comforting meals came from. Regardless of our situation and how sad something felt, a big bowl of food that had been made with love just seemed to make everything feel better for a short while.

glug of olive oil
1 red onion, peeled and finely chopped
4 garlic cloves, peeled and finely chopped
1 tsp garlic salt
500g (1lb 2oz) 10%-fat minced
   (ground) beef
1 x 400g (14oz) tin chopped tomatoes
3 fresh chillies, finely chopped
   (deseeded if you prefer)
2 tsp ground cumin
2 tsp paprika
pinch of ground black pepper
2 beef stock cubes
200ml (6¾fl oz/1 cup) milk
1 x 400g (14oz) tin red kidney beans

EQUIPMENT
chopping board—knife—large deep frying
pan—wooden spoon

SOFTEN THE ONION AND BROWN THE MINCE
Heat the oil in a frying pan over medium heat, add the onion and cook gently until soft and translucent – cooking it low and slow gives a beautiful hum to this gorgeous dish. Add the garlic cloves and garlic salt and cook for another minute then add the mince and let it sizzle and brown, breaking it up with a wooden spoon.

ADD THE REMAINING INGREDIENTS AND SIMMER
Add the chopped tomatoes and chillies and throw in the cumin, salt, pepper and paprika. Crumble in the two beef stock cubes (without water – we are trying to get an intense and condensed flavour, the water will just dilute the flavours). This next step sounds strange – when I first saw Dad do it I was concerned – but he swears it's the secret to the best chilli: pour in a cup of milk (the addition of milk to enrich a meat dish is traditional in some cuisines e.g. some traditional Italian Bolognese. The more I have thought about this I can understand why it would work, I think the milk negates some of the spiciness from the chillies, but it leaves the flavours and the warmth.). Simmer for as long as possible. Dad says the longer it cooks the better: if you can make it in the morning and let it cook low and slow until dinner time, do it. Twenty minutes before serving, chuck in the kidney beans!

SERVE
We throw the usual bland rice and/or jacket potato out the window – the only way to eat this is with a big white French baguette. Yup, you heard it, we eat this with a loaf of bread. I told you we do comfort food. Layer a slice of soft (tiger bread is my favourite) baguette with butter then layer on that chilli! Just try this as an easy weeknight dinner; it really does warm the soul!

Roast Chicken
Midweek Traybake

SERVES 4

An English roast dinner is like a hug that sets you up for the week. I don't know why we limit ourselves to just having it on a Sunday because really, a roast dinner is one of the easiest things to make and you can forget about it while it's in the oven. It's easy to double up, too, leaving you plenty of leftovers for the rest of the week. Getting these staple ingredients in the cupboard and fridge really does help you out when you're looking for comfort food and ease.

olive oil, for drizzling
600g (1lb 5oz) potatoes, peeled and cut into bite-sized pieces
250g (9oz) parsnips, peeled and cut into bite-sized pieces
250g (9oz) carrots, peeled and cut into bite-sized pieces
250g (9oz) Brussels sprouts, trimmed and halved
12 skin on, boneless chicken thighs
250ml (8fl oz/1 cup) chicken stock (bouillon)
1 tsp garlic granules or powder
1 tsp onion granules or powder
1 tsp thyme
1 tsp rosemary
1 tsp salt
1 tsp freshly ground black pepper
2–4 tbsp runny honey

EQUIPMENT
chopping board—knife—large baking dish

PREHEAT THE OVEN
Preheat the oven to 180°C (160°C fan/350°F/gas mark 4).

ARRANGE EVERYTHING IN THE DISH
Generously drizzle some oil in the base of the baking dish then add a layer of potatoes (basically, we want the ingredients that need the longest cooking time at the bottom so the juice from the chicken drips onto them, helping them to cook). Add the parsnips, then the carrots and then the Brussels sprouts, then place the chicken thighs on top of all of this, skin side up. Pour the chicken stock over everything then drizzle with more oil before sprinkling on the garlic granules, onion granules, thyme, rosemary, salt and pepper. Finally, drizzle the honey over everything.

ROAST AND SERVE
Pop the dish in the oven for 30–40 minutes, until everything is succulent and cooked. Serve and enjoy. Leftovers can be portioned up and stored in the fridge for up to 3 days as a yummy meal prep filled with veggies and protein.

ALTERNATIVE INGREDIENTS
Chicken thighs: use lamb chops
Herbs and spices: use sage and a sprinkle of nutmeg
Sprouts: they're an excellent vegetable to use here because they cook at the same time as other veggies. Drizzled in honey and with the juices from the chicken I would be surprised if you didn't enjoy them.
Make it veggie or vegan: remove the chicken all together, or use a chicken substitute, swapping the chicken stock for vegetable stock. If making it vegan, swap the honey for maple syrup.

BAKING EVER

YTHING BETTER

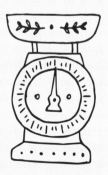

The Beavis
Traditional Tiffin

This tiffin originated when I was in sixth form (senior year). For at least 6 months, my sister would ask me to make it once every 2 weeks, and she still asks for it every now and again. There is absolutely NOTHING good for you in this tiffin, it's jam packed with naughties, but sometimes, when you're going through a tough time or feeling blue, you don't want something good for you, you want something that leaves you and your sweet tooth completely satisfied. This is it.

150g (5½oz) salted butter
3 tbsp caster (superfine) sugar
3 tbsp golden syrup
6 tsp cocoa powder
250g (9oz) digestive biscuits
150g (5½oz) mini marshmallows
100g (3½oz) any spare chocolate or sweets
   that you may want to throw in
100g (3½oz) white chocolate
100g (3½oz) milk chocolate

EQUIPMENT
saucepan—spoon—freezer bag—rolling
pin—large mixing bowl—20cm (8in)
square cake tin—baking parchment—knife
or toothpick

LET'S GET MELTING
Gently melt the butter in a saucepan over a low heat, then add the sugar and golden syrup. Mix together until the sugar has dissolved then mix in the cocoa powder until smooth. Take it off the heat and pour into a large mixing bowl.

PREP THE OTHER INGREDIENTS
Pop the biscuits into a freezer bag and bash with a rolling pin to roughly break them up. When your butter mixture is melted, add the biscuits, marshmallows and any other chocolate bits that you have lying around the house and mix to coat. Pour this into a tin lined with baking parchment and press it down.

DRIZZLE WITH CHOCOLATE AND SET
To finish the tiffin, melt the white chocolate and milk chocolate separately. Pour the milk chocolate onto the tiffin and then drizzle the white chocolate over that. Drag a knife or toothpick through the chocolate to create a feathered pattern on the top. Pop it in the fridge to set for a couple of hours and then slice into slabs and enjoy with a cup of tea.

ALTERNATIVE INGREDIENTS
You can make this recipe your own by using any fillings you like. Add raisins, nuts, your favourite biscuits... whatever you fancy! I occasionally melt some Biscoff or Nutella and swirl that into the topping too. This is the perfect recipe to make around Easter to use up all of the Easter eggs and chocolate.

BAKING EVERYTHING BETTER

Paddington Marmalade Cake

In the British countryside, marmalade on toast fixes almost anything. Muddy fields and muddier animals? Come on in, sit down and have a cup of tea and some marmalade on toast. When Paddington Bear is hungry, or if things seem a little grey, he pulls a marmalade sandwich from his hat. With this in mind I wanted to create a marmalade cake, something sweet, sticky and citrusy to make us feel all warm and fuzzy inside. Think lemon drizzle cake with a stickier twist.

170g (5¾oz) salted butter, softened
170g (5¾oz/¾ cup) caster (superfine) sugar
3 medium eggs
grated zest and juice of 1 large orange
1 tsp vanilla extract
5 tbsp orange marmalade, plus an extra 2 tbsp for the top
285g (10oz/2¼ cups) self-raising (self-rising) flour

EQUIPMENT
grater—900g (2lb) loaf tin—parchment (optional)mixing bowl—electric whisk or wooden spoon—skewer or toothpick

PREHEAT THE OVEN AND PREPARE THE TIN
Preheat the oven to 180°C (160°C fan/350°F/gas mark 4) and line the base and sides or grease the loaf tin.

MAKE THE SPONGE MIX
Cream the butter and sugar in a bowl until light and fluffy, then add the eggs, one at a time, beating after each addition. Add the orange zest and juice and mix, then add the vanilla, marmalade and flour and give it a final mix so you have a lovely thick batter.

BAKING TIME
Spoon the batter into the lined or greased loaf tin and bake in the oven for about 35–45 minutes until golden brown and risen and a skewer comes out clean.

GLAZE THE CAKE
When the cake comes out of the oven, make little holes in the top of it with a skewer or toothpick and spread the extra tablespoons of marmalade on top. It will melt due to the heat of the cake and seep into the cake, leaving a sticky orange glaze on top.

SERVE
Slice and serve with a cup of tea.

The cake will keep in a cake tin or sealed container for about 3 days at room temperature, or up to 5 days in a container in the fridge.

ALTERNATIVE INGREDIENTS
Butter: use margarine or baking spread

My Countryside Apple Pie

I have always loved apple crumble, but I also love pastry on any kind of fruit tart. I found with apple pies that have a shortcrust pastry top and base, the pastry always seemed to fall away from the apple, which doesn't happen with crumble, so I created this countryside apple pie with the classic shortcrust base and a crumble topping so you get the best of both worlds. You can make the pie the day before serving, storing it unbaked in the fridge covered in cling film (plastic wrap).

1 x 320g (11¼oz) sheet of shortcrust (pie) pastry
clotted cream or custard, to serve

FOR THE FILLING
700g (1lb 9oz) eating apples, cored, peeled and thinly sliced (as thin as a £1 coin)
125g (4¼oz/⅔ cup) light brown sugar
1 tsp ground cinnamon
pinch of ground nutmeg
1 tsp cornflour (cornstarch)

FOR THE CRUMBLE
120g (4¼oz/1 cup) plain (all-purpose) flour
60g (2¼oz/generous ¼ cup) granulated sugar
60g (2¼oz/⅓ cup) light brown sugar
80g (2¾oz) cold butter, cubed, plus extra for greasing the pie dish if needed

EQUIPMENT
20cm (8in) pie dish (ideally non-stick)
fork—deep, large saucepan or frying pan (big enough to cook the apples in)—bowl

PREHEAT THE OVEN AND BLIND-BAKE THE PASTRY

Preheat the oven to 180°C (160°C fan/350˚F/gas mark 4). Grease the pie dish with butter if it's not non-stick. Place the pastry sheet in the dish and push into the edges, crimping it around the sides and allowing it to overhang. Prick a few holes in the bottom with a fork and line the pastry with parchment and fill it with rice or baking beans to avoid the pastry rising in the middle. Bake in the oven for 10 minutes then remove from the oven and set aside (this helps avoid your pie having that infamous 'soggy bottom'). Once the pastry is cool, trim off the excess overhanging pastry.

STEW THE APPLES

Put the sliced apples, brown sugar, cinnamon, nutmeg and the cornflour in the saucepan and cook over a medium-low heat for 5–10 minutes, stirring occasionally, being careful not to burn the sugar – you want the apples to slowly soften.

MAKE THE CRUMBLE TOP

While the apples are cooking, put the flour and both sugars for the crumble topping in a bowl and mix with your hand, then add the cubed butter and rub with your fingertips until the mixture resembles breadcrumbs.

ASSEMBLE AND BAKE THE PIE

Scoop the apples into the pastry shell, sprinkle the crumble mix over the top and bake in the oven for 20–25 minutes until golden brown and the pie crust is cooked through.

SERVE

Serve with a dollop of clotted cream, ice cream or custard for a hearty, warming dessert!

ALTERNATIVE INGREDIENTS
Apples: use pear. My nana likes to throw in some blackberries alongside the apple!

'Heaven in my Mouth' Pumpkin Pies

MAKES ONE 20CM (8IN) PUMPKIN PIE

I make pumpkin pie every autumn. One autumn I made them for my partner's 6-year-old niece who is probably my toughest critic. When Darcey had one and said 'this is heaven in my mouth' I knew I had to share the recipe with everyone! So, guys, you can thank her for this. It's one of the scrummiest things to make, especially if you finish it with a generous dollop of whipped cream.

1 x 320g (11¼oz) sheet of shortcrust (pie) pastry
3 large eggs
165g (5¾oz/generous ¾ cup) light brown sugar
425g (15oz) pumpkin (squash) puree
175ml (6fl oz/¾ cup) double (heavy) cream
2 tsp ground cinnamon
1 tsp ground ginger
whipped cream, to serve

EQUIPMENT
20cm (8in) pie dish or tart tin (non-stick, if you want to take it out of the dish to serve)
bowl—fork

PREHEAT THE OVEN AND BAKE THE CRUST
Preheat the oven to 180°C (160°C fan/350°F/gas mark 4). Unroll the pastry and pop it in the tart tin or pie dish, pushing it into the corners of the tin and poking little holes with a fork in the base of the pastry. Bake in the oven for 10 minutes until lightly brown and less oily.

MAKE THE PUMPKIN FILLING AND BAKE
While the crust bakes, make the filling. Mix the eggs, brown sugar, pumpkin puree, double cream, cinnamon and ginger in a bowl. Yep, it really is that easy. Pour this into the baked pastry base and bake for about 40 minutes, until the filling has set.

SLICE AND SERVE
Remove from the oven and serve sliced (warm or cold), with a dollop of whipped cream on top.

The pie will keep in the fridge in an airtight container for up to 3 days.

Grandparents-approved Carrot Cake

MAKES ONE THREE-
LAYER CAKE

Nana and Gramps have had a lot of carrot cake in their time, but I still stand by the fact that Gramps said this is the best one he has ever had (this is coming from the man who will tell me if something is too sweet, although when it comes to my desserts they are usually 'just right'). So, without further ado, here is my higgledy piggledy three-layer carrot cake.

230ml (7¾fl oz/scant 1 cup) vegetable oil
100g (3½oz) full-fat Greek yoghurt
4 medium eggs
2 tsp vanilla extract
250g (9oz/2¼ cups) self-raising
   (self-rising) flour
15g (½oz) ground almonds (almond meal)
335g (12oz/2 cups) soft light brown sugar
2 tsp ground cinnamon
a pinch of ground nutmeg
3 carrots, peeled and finely grated
100g (3½oz) walnuts, roughly chopped
100g (3½oz) pecans, roughly chopped
a few chopped nuts (I like walnuts),
   to decorate

PREHEAT THE OVEN AND PREPARE THE TINS
Preheat the oven to 200°C (180°C fan/400°F/gas mark 6) and generously grease each tin with butter or oil.

MAKE THE CAKE BATTER
Put all the wet ingredients (the oil, Greek yoghurt, eggs and vanilla) in a large bowl or stand mixer and whisk to combine. Combine the dry ingredients (the flour, ground almonds, brown sugar, cinnamon and nutmeg) in a separate bowl. Mix the dry ingredients into the bowl containing the wet ingredients until the mixture has no lumps, then fold in the grated carrots and chopped nuts.

BAKE THE CAKES
Divide the mixture evenly between the prepared cake tins and bake on the middle shelf of the oven for 25 minutes, or until a skewer inserted into the middle of the cakes comes out clean (or gently press the top of each cake – they should spring back). Remove from the oven and turn out onto a wire rack. Set aside to cool.

recipe continued

FOR THE CREAM CHEESE BUTTERCREAM
225g (8oz) salted butter at room
    temperature
200g (7oz) soft full-fat cream cheese
2 tsp vanilla extract
600g (1lb 5oz/6 cups) icing
    (confectioners') sugar

EQUIPMENT
3 x 20cm (8in) cake tins—weighing
scales—peeler—2 large bowls—electric
whisk, stand mixer —wooden spoon

MAKE THE BUTTERCREAM

Put the butter in a bowl and whisk with an electric whisk or in the bowl of a stand mixer for about 5 minutes until fluffy and pale. Add the cream cheese and vanilla extract and mix again then gradually add the icing sugar, tablespoon by tablespoon, whilst whisking continuously. When you have a smooth creamy mixture and your cakes are completely cooled you're ready to start icing them!

ASSEMBLE THE CAKE

Sandwich the cakes with a thick layer of the cream cheese buttercream, then cover the top of the cake with the remaining buttercream and sprinkle with the remaining chopped nuts. Have a slice with a cup of tea at that 3–4 o'clock spot where we all have a little energy dip!

ALTERNATIVE INGREDIENTS
Vegetable oil: use sunflower oil or other flavourless oil
Greek yoghurt: use plain yoghurt
Soft light brown sugar: use another brown sugar (white sugar burns a little too easily)
Walnuts/pecans: use any nut you fancy. Walnuts are traditional but I throw a few pecans in there too because they're less bitter and my sister prefers them over my mum's favourite, the walnut.

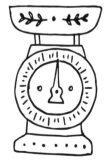

Chocolate & Hazelnut
Croissant Pudding

SERVES 8

Nutella, chocolate and hazelnuts are a tough combination to beat, so throw it all in a pudding with some croissants and a few other yummy bits and pieces and you have a delicious show-stopper pudding perfect for any party (or a Sunday afternoon treat!).

Make the pudding a couple of hours in advance, cover and chill until you're ready to bake it and serve!

2 tbsp butter
6 croissants, halved lengthways (as if you were going to make a sandwich with them)
4 medium eggs
4 tbsp light brown sugar
250ml (8fl oz/1 cup) whole (full-fat) milk
250ml (8fl oz/1 cup) double (heavy) cream
2 tsp vanilla extract
4 tbsp Nutella, melted
200g (7oz) chocolate chips of your choice (I like a mixture of dark, milk and white)
a large handful of roughly chopped blanched hazelnuts
ice cream or double (heavy) cream, to serve

EQUIPMENT
chopping board—knife—ovenproof dish or skillet—bowl or jug—hand whisk

PREHEAT THE OVEN AND GREASE THE DISH
Preheat the oven to 180°C (160°C fan/350°F/gas mark 4) and grease the ovenproof dish or skillet with the butter.

START ASSEMBLING THE PUDDING
Lay the croissant pieces against one another in your dish.

MAKE THE CUSTARD MIX
Put the eggs, brown sugar, milk, cream, vanilla extract and Nutella in a bowl or jug and whisk until smooth.

FINISH ASSEMBLING THE PUDDING AND BAKE
Sprinkle half the chocolate chips and hazelnuts over the croissants in your dish then pour over the custard mix, then add the remaining chocolate chips and hazelnuts on top. Bake the pudding in the oven for 15–20 minutes until golden brown and the liquid has set.

SERVE
Now, the real question is are you going to serve it with ice cream or double cream? Enjoy!

Any leftovers will keep happily in the fridge for up to 24 hours.

ALTERNATIVE INGREDIENTS
Croissants: go for something a little sweeter than just white bread such as brioche or waffles
Chocolate chips: use white chocolate, dark chocolate or milk chocolate or chunks of your favourite chocolate bar. Get creative
Hazelnuts: use walnuts, pistachios, almonds or pecans
Nutella: use melted peanut butter to make a Snickers-style pudding, or use white chocolate spread

Poppy Seed, Rosemary & Lemon Drizzle Muffins

I love lemon drizzle cake. It's a staple in our house and one of my mum's favourite bakes, so I often whip up a simple lemon drizzle or a lemon curd cake and they go within hours of being baked! There is something satisfying about lemon in a cake because it can be made throughout the seasons: in the summer it makes a wonderful dessert to have with a sorbet or ice cream, and in the winter a muffin makes the perfect snack to go with a warm cup of tea.

350g (12½oz) salted butter or margarine, softened
350g (12½oz/1½ cups) caster (superfine) sugar
5 medium eggs
350g (12½oz/2½ cups) self-raising flour
grated zest and juice of 2 lemons, plus 1 extra lemon to decorate
2 tbsp poppy seeds
4 rosemary sprigs (1 for the cake, 3 to decorate)

FOR THE ICING
180g (6¼oz/1½ cups) icing (powdered) sugar
5–6 tbsp lemon juice

EQUIPMENT
12-hole muffin tin (and 12 muffin cases if it's not non-stick)—mixing bowl — wooden spoon or electric whisk—chopping board knife—little bowl

PREHEAT THE OVEN AND PREPARE THE TIN
Preheat the oven to 180°C (160°C fan/350°F/gas mark 4) and line the muffin tin with paper cases or just grease the holes with butter if it's non-stick.

MAKE THE BATTER
Put the butter and sugar in the mixing bowl and beat with a spoon or an electric whisk until pale and fluffy. Add the eggs, one at a time, beating after each addition, then fold in the flour. Add the juice and zest from the 2 lemons and throw in the poppy seeds. Pull the leaves off one of the rosemary sprigs, chop them up really finely and add to the batter too. Mix well so the poppy seeds, lemon and rosemary are all incorporated evenly throughout the batter.

BAKE THE MUFFINS
Spoon the batter evenly into the muffin tin holes or cases and bake in the oven for about 25 minutes until golden brown. If you press the top of one, the sponge should spring back (and a skewer inserted into a muffin will come out clean).

MAKE THE ICING
While your muffins are in the oven, mix the icing sugar and lemon juice together to create a thick smooth icing.

ICE THE MUFFINS AND SERVE
Remove the muffins from the oven and leave to cool, spoon over the icing, sprinkle over some rosemary leaves and grate over some lemon zest. That's it, pretty muffins made for any season!

The muffins will keep in a sealed container for about 3 days at room temperature, or up to 5 days in a container in the fridge.

ALTERNATIVE INGREDIENTS
Lemons: use the zest and juice of an orange for a lovely twist
Poppy seeds: use chia seeds
Rosemary: use fresh thyme leaves or mint leaves

White Chocolate & Raspberry Waffle Pudding

SERVES 6 (GENEROUSLY)

When I went to coffee shops as a child I always begged for a white chocolate and raspberry muffin – there's something about tart raspberry and sweet white chocolate that just WORKS, always has, always will. I've never really liked the texture of bread in classic bread and butter pudding, so I wondered what would happen if I swapped the bread for waffles... And thus, this white chocolate and raspberry pudding was created.

1–2 tbsp butter, for greasing
500g (1lb 2oz) shop-bought thick waffles, cut into large, bite-sized pieces
250g (9oz) fresh raspberries
150g (5½oz) white chocolate chips (or chopped white chocolate)
300ml (10fl oz/1¼ cups) whole (full-fat) milk
300ml (10fl oz/1¼ cups) double (heavy) cream
2 tbsp caster (superfine) sugar
2 tsp vanilla extract
3 large eggs
icing (powdered) sugar, for dusting

EQUIPMENT
chopping board—knife—26cm (10in) ovenproof dish—bowl or jug—hand whisk

PREHEAT THE OVEN AND GREASE THE DISH
Preheat the oven to 180°C (160°C fan/350˚F/gas mark 4) and grease the ovenproof dish with the butter, making sure you get in all of those corners.

START ASSEMBLING THE PUDDING
Throw a handful of waffle pieces into the dish, along with a few raspberries and a sprinkling of white chocolate pieces and repeat until they are all used up.

MAKE THE CUSTARD MIX
Put the milk, cream, sugar, vanilla extract and eggs in a bowl or a jug and whisk until smooth, then pour this evenly over your pudding.

BAKE THE PUDDING
Bake the pudding in the oven for 25–30 minutes until golden brown (keep an eye on it – white chocolate burns quickly and you don't want any burnt pieces on top).

SERVE
Remove from the oven and allow to cool slightly, then dust with icing sugar, serve and enjoy this lip-smackingly good pudding

ALTERNATIVE INGREDIENTS
Waffles: use stale white bread (I use croissants for a chocolate and hazelnut pudding on page 184 and they work especially well), avoid seeded or brown breads
Raspberries: use strawberries, blueberries, banana or apricot. Anything tart that complements the chocolate is a wonderful go-to (get creative!)
Whole (full-fat) milk/ double (heavy) cream: use single (light) cream or a shop-bought custard

Nectarine &
Almond Tart

This tart is so easy and versatile. I love to make it on a summer's morning or a summer's afternoon after a barbecue – it's the perfect way to start or end your day. Anything baked on a sheet of puff pastry always feels like a warm hug to me – because puff pastry is made by folding pastry over butter over and over again there is something utterly delicious about those flaky layers – and I love mixing up the fruit and nuts to make it different each time. Nectarine and almonds are one of my favourite combinations (another crowd-pleaser is pistachio, white chocolate and raspberries).

1 x 320g (11¼oz) sheet of all-butter
    puff pastry
100g (3½oz) shop-bought custard
20–30g (¾–1oz) ground almonds (almond
    meal)
3 nectarines, stoned and thinly sliced
a handful of flaked (slivered) almonds
1 tbsp apricot jam
1–2 tbsp icing (powdered) sugar
clotted cream or crème fraiche, to serve

EQUIPMENT
chopping board—knife—baking tray
baking parchment (if your pastry doesn't
come with it)—bowl—pastry brush

PREHEAT THE OVEN AND LINE THE BAKING TRAY
Preheat the oven to 200°C (180°C fan/400°F/gas mark 6). Line a baking tray with the paper under the shop-bought pastry (if it comes with it) or line it with parchment. Lay the pastry on it.

SCORE THE PASTRY
Score a border 2cm (¾in) inside the edge of the pastry with the blunt edge of your knife, making sure that you don't cut through the pastry.

TOP THE PASTRY
Mix the custard and ground almonds in a bowl, then evenly spread the mix inside the square you scored. Scatter the thinly sliced nectarines on top of the custard and and sprinkle over the flaked almonds.

BAKE
Brush the edges of the pastry with the apricot jam and bake in the oven for 10–15 minutes, until the edges are puffed up and golden. Remove from the oven, sprinkle with the icing sugar, slice, and enjoy with your favourite cream,

ALTERNATIVE INGREDIENTS
Puff pastry: use shortcrust (pie) pastry
Almonds: use crushed pistachios, hazelnuts, pecans or cashews
Nectarines: use anything slightly tart that has a tickle of sweetness, such as strawberries, raspberries, pear, apple, peach, pineapple or even passionfruit. The list really is endless and it's wonderful to experiment.

Banana, Peanut Butter & Chocolate Muffins

MAKES 6 LARGE MUFFINS

Like most of my recipes there was no rhyme or reason behind this. I had moved into my partner's flat and he didn't have a loaf tin for me to make banana bread in, but he did have a muffin tin, so I thought 'ooo, let's make muffins'. There were four half-empty tubs of peanut butter in his cupboard and some half-eaten chocolate bars strewn about the fridge, so I created banana muffins with chocolate chips and an oozy peanut butter middle. Needless to say, within 12 hours all 6 large muffins had been devoured!

2 ripe bananas

150g (5½oz) salted butter, softened

150g (5½oz/⅔ cup) caster
    (superfine) sugar

150g (5½oz/1¼ cups) self-raising
    (self-rising) flour

2 medium eggs

1 tsp baking powder

100g (3½oz) chocolate chips of
    your choice

6–7 tsp smooth peanut butter

EQUIPMENT
bowl—spoon—fork—wooden spoon
6-hole muffin tin—6 muffin cases (if using a non-stick tin)

PREHEAT THE OVEN AND MAKE THE BATTER
Preheat the oven to 180°C (160°C fan/350˚F/gas mark 4). Peel the bananas and mash them in a bowl with the back of a fork, then add the butter and sugar and mix until pale and fluffy. Add both eggs and mix before throwing in your flour and baking powder. Mix once more until you have a smooth batter then fold in the chocolate chips until they're evenly spread throughout the batter.

MAKE THAT OOZY PB MIDDLE
To your muffin cases or non-stick muffin tin add 1 tablespoon of the muffin batter, then add a teaspoon of peanut butter on top and then another tablespoon of the muffin batter. Repeat this process until you have used up all of your mixture.

BAKE THE MUFFINS
Bake the muffins in the oven for 15–18 minutes. When the muffins spring back if you press the top, they're done (the skewer test won't work here because the gooey peanut butter centre will mean it won't come out clean).

SERVE
Remove from the oven and serve. The best way to eat these is when they are warm out of the oven while the chocolate is melted and the peanut butter is oozy.

The muffins will keep in a cake tin or sealed container for about 3 days at room temperature, or up to 5 days in a container in the fridge.

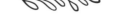

ALTERNATIVE INGREDIENTS
Peanut butter: use your favourite spread (being the child I am, a little Nutella in each one works so well)

Chocolate chips: for something a little more nutritious add a few nuts to the batter (just halve the chocolate quantities and add the same amount of nuts). I love hazelnuts, almonds and pecans

Honey & Almond Bundt Cake
– a Proper Countryside Treat

Milk and honey is my countryside comfort. When I was a little girl, my mum gave me warm honey and milk to help me go to sleep and get me settled. I wanted to recreate this sensation that we all have at some point in our childhood, in cake form (well, why not, cake makes everything better). Baking cakes in a bundt tin is so effective: you don't need to decorate them with anything fancy as they look beautiful as they are. This is the cake tin I pull out when I am feeling lazy.

150g (5½oz) salted butter, softened, plus extra for greasing
115g (4oz/scant ⅔ cup) brown sugar
2 medium eggs
100g (3½oz/generous ¾ cup) self-raising (self-rising) flour
100g (3½oz/⅔ cup) ground almonds (almond meal)
120g (4¼oz) runny honey
1 tsp vanilla extract
30g (1oz) milk
crème fraîche or cream, to serve (optional)
honey, to serve (optional)

EQUIPMENT
20cm (8in) bundt (ring) tin (or a 900g (2lb) loaf tin or muffin tin: use whatever you have)—bowl—wooden spoon or electric whisk

PREHEAT THE OVEN AND PREPARE THE TIN
Preheat the oven to 180°C (160°C fan/350°F/gas mark 4). Grease the tin with butter and make sure you get into all those corners, so the cake comes out perfectly formed.

MAKE THE CAKE BATTER
Beat the butter and sugar with a wooden spoon or electric whisk until smooth and fluffy, then add the eggs one at a time, beating well after each addition until incorporated, then mix in the flour and ground almonds. Add the honey, vanilla and milk and give it one final mix.

LET THE MAGIC HAPPEN
Spoon the batter into the prepared tin and bake in the oven for 20–25 minutes (15–20 minutes if you're using a muffin tin) until golden brown and springy to the touch. Remove from the oven and leave to cool, then turn it upside down: a beautifully simple sponge cake should pop out! Serve with crème fraîche or cream and honey.

The cake will keep in a cake tin or sealed container for about 3 days at room temperature, or up to 5 days in a container in the fridge.

Nana's Chocolate Cake

MAKES 1 X 18CM (7IN) CAKE

This recipe is very special to me. When my sister and I were little, Nana and Gramps looked after us a lot and one of my key memories is coming home to a cup of tea and a slice of Nana's chocolate cake. My sister and I would fight over who had more buttercream filling in their cake and we would try and nab the biggest slice. No matter what was happening at home, a slice of Nana's chocolate cake in front of the telly with something warm after school would always make us feel better. We could focus on our homework and after-school activities better because we had a big chocolatey grin on our faces. So, Nana, if you're reading this, you were our superstar and Gramps, thanks for letting us eat your portions of cake!

170g (5¾oz) margarine (Nana calls it cooking fat), plus extra for greasing
170g (5¾oz/1½ cups) self-raising (self-rising) flour
2 heaped tbsp cocoa powder
1 tsp baking powder
170g (5¾oz/generous ¾ cup) caster (superfine) sugar
3 large eggs

FOR THE CHOCOLATE ICING
60g (2¼oz) margarine
120g (4¼oz/1¼ cups) icing (powdered) sugar
60g (2¼oz) cocoa powder

EQUIPMENT
2 x 18cm (7in) cake tins—2 large bowls—sieve—electric whisk (or, traditionally, a wooden spoon)—wire rack

PREHEAT THE OVEN AND PREPARE THE TINS
Preheat the oven to 200°C (180°C fan/400°F/gas mark 6) and grease the cake tins with margarine.

MAKE THE CAKE BATTER
Put the margarine in a large bowl and beat with an electric whisk or wooden spoon until smooth and creamy. Sift in the flour, cocoa powder, baking powder and then add the caster sugar and eggs. Mix with a wooden spoon until smooth and creamy.

BAKE THE CAKES
Divide the mixture evenly between the prepared cake tins and bake on the middle shelf of the oven for 25 minutes, or until a skewer inserted into the middle of the cakes comes out clean (or gently press the top of each cake – they should spring back). Remove from the oven, carefully turn out onto a wire rack and leave to cool.

MAKE THE CHOCOLATE ICING
Put the margarine in a bowl and whisk with an electric whisk until fluffy and pale. Sift in the icing sugar and cocoa powder and mix it in, making sure there are no lumps and that the icing has a spreadable consistency.

ASSEMBLE THE CAKE
Sandwich the cakes with the icing (when one of us had done well in school, Nana used to double the chocolate filling and pop another layer on top... but that was only for special occasions).

Peaches & Cream
with a Crumble Top

SERVES 4

When you crave comfort food in the
summer, you don't want to be slaving
in the kitchen when it's hot outside, so
this pudding is perfect: it takes minutes,
everyone loves it and the crumble topping
and vanilla cream can both be made in
advance, so you just need two minutes to
caramelise your peaches and that is it!
Make the crumble topping and the vanilla
cream up to 24 hours in advance (storing
them in the fridge), so all you need to do
before serving is spend a few minutes
caramelising your peaches.

4 peaches, halved and stones removed
1 tbsp soft light brown sugar
100g (3½oz) salted butter

FOR THE CRUMBLE TOPPING
50g (1¾oz/generous ⅓ cup) plain (all-
    purpose) flour
20g (¾oz) caster (superfine) sugar
25g (1oz) rolled (porridge) oats
35g (1¼oz) cold butter, diced

FOR THE VANILLA CREAM
200ml (7fl oz/generous ¾ cup) double
    (heavy) cream
1 tbsp icing (powdered) sugar
2 tsp vanilla extract
100g (3½oz) mascarpone

EQUIPMENT
2 mixing bowls—baking tray—electric
whisk—frying pan

PREHEAT THE OVEN AND MAKE THE CRUMBLE MIX
Preheat the oven to 180°C (160°C fan/350°F/gas mark 4). Mix
the flour, sugar and oats in a bowl then add the butter and rub it
into the dry ingredients with your fingertips to a crumble texture.
Spread the crumb across a baking tray evenly and bake in the oven
for 10 minutes or so until golden brown and crunchy with big
pieces and little pieces). Remove from the oven and set aside.

MAKE THE VANILLA CREAM
Whisk the cream in a bowl until thickened, then add the icing
sugar and vanilla and whisk briefly before adding the mascarpone
and giving it a final whip.

MAKE THOSE PEACHES GOLDEN
Dip each peach half flesh side down in the brown sugar. Melt the
butter in the frying pan over a medium heat and once the butter is
browning slightly add the peaches sugared side down. Cook for 1–2
minutes until they caramelise and turn golden brown then flip and
cook for a further 1–2 minutes on the other side (this makes sure
they're warm through and all their juices are warm and sweet).

SERVE
Plate the peaches with a dollop of the vanilla cream and sprinkle
over the crumble topping!

ALTERNATIVE INGREDIENTS
Peaches: use pears, nectarines or handfuls of berries

Cinnamon Crunch Cake

This recipe came about thanks to my childhood crumble-loving era! Every Sunday, the pudding after our family roast dinner would be a variation of crumble (our favourite was apple and blackberry) – as little children, my sister and I would sit there just eating the sugary crunchy crumble part. I wanted to make a cake that had this on top, so you can enjoy the yummiest bit of crumble WITH cake! Is there anything better?

FOR THE CRUNCHY TOP
45g (1½oz/¼ cup) soft light brown sugar
45g (1½oz/scant ¼ cup) granulated sugar
1 tsp ground cinnamon
pinch of salt
180g (6¼oz/1½ cups) plain
    (all-purpose) flour
120g (4¼oz) salted butter, melted

FOR THE CAKE
120g (4¼oz) salted butter, softened
100g (3½oz/generous ½ cup) soft
    light brown sugar
90g (3oz) full-fat Greek yoghurt
4 tbsp whole (full-fat) milk
2 tsp vanilla extract
180g (6¼oz/1½ cups) self-raising flour
½ tsp ground cinnamon
pinch of salt

EQUIPMENT
20–23cm (8–9in) cake tin—parchment
2 mixing bowls—electric whisk or
wooden spoon

PREHEAT THE OVEN AND PREPARE THE CAKE TIN
Preheat the oven to 180°C (160°C fan/350°F/gas mark 4) and line a 20–23cm (8–9in) cake tin with parchment.

MAKE THE CRUMBLE TOPPING
Mix the sugars, cinnamon, salt and flour in a bowl then pour over the melted butter and mix with your fingertips, a wooden spoon or an electric whisk for a minute or two until you have a crumbly mixture. Pop to one side while you make the cake batter.

MAKE THE CAKE
Cream the butter and sugar together in a large bowl until light and fluffy. Stir together the yoghurt, milk and vanilla extract in a small bowl. Pour the yoghurt mixture into the butter and sugar and stir to combine. Fold in the flour, cinnamon and salt then spread the batter into the lined tin. Sprinkle the crumbs on top (keep as many of them as large as possible, so they stick and don't crumble off the cake as soon as you take a bite).

BAKE!
Bake the cake in the oven for about 40 minutes, until a skewer inserted into the cake comes out clean. Let it cool, slice and enjoy!

The cake will keep in a cake tin or sealed container for about 3 days at room temperature, or up to 5 days in a container in the fridge.

Blueberry &
Orange Slice

SERVES 8

I accidentally made this during the first lockdown: we had oranges and blueberries that needed eating and I fancied baking something! The citrus and little bites of tart blueberries encased in a gorgeous sponge were delicious, and the ground almonds made it even more moist. It's an absolute winner and in the summertime it's such a lovely treat.

100g (3½oz) salted butter, softened
100g (3½oz/generous ⅓ cup) caster (superfine) sugar
1 medium egg
115ml (3¾fl oz/½ cup) whole (full-fat) milk
100g (3½oz/ generous ¾ cup) plain (all-purpose) flour
100g (3½oz/⅔ cup) ground almonds (almond meal)
2 tsp baking powder
grated zest of 1 large orange
4 tbsp orange juice
2–3 large handfuls of blueberries
icing (powdered) sugar, for dusting

EQUIPMENT
20cm (8in) loose-bottomed tart tin or cake tin—mixing bowl—hand-held electric whisk—wooden spoon—grater

PREHEAT THE OVEN AND PREPARE THE CAKE TIN
Preheat the oven to 180°C (160°C fan/350°F/gas mark 4) and grease the tart or cake tin.

MAKE THE CAKE
Cream the butter and sugar in a bowl until pale and fluffy, then add egg and milk and mix until well incorporated. Fold in the flour, ground almonds and baking powder. When your batter is smooth and lump-free, add the orange zest, orange juice and blueberries and carefully fold the fruit through, being careful not to break too many blueberries or you'll have a dull purple sponge! Transfer the batter to the prepared tin and bake for 15–18 minutes until golden brown and risen beautifully.

SERVE
Remove the sponge from the oven and allow to cool slightly before dusting with icing sugar. Serve and enjoy as a beautiful dessert or tea-time snack!

The cake will keep in a cake tin or sealed container for about 3 days at room temperature, or up to 5 days in a container in the fridge.

ALTERNATIVE INGREDIENTS
Orange: use other citrus fruit – lemon works well
Blueberries: use any berry, such as raspberries

BAKING EVERYTHING BETTER **201**

Big Kids Kinder Nutella Cheesecake

I am yet to meet anyone who doesn't like Kinder Bueno (yes, I am talking about adults too). The indulgent treat takes me back to being a kid and eating Kinder's Happy Hippos on the way back from school – I loved the combination of wafer, chocolate and hazelnut spread. We have probably all heard of Biscoff cheesecake (everyone was making their own version in lockdown), but here is my Kinder Bueno no-bake 6-ingredient cheesecake. It tastes out of this world!

250g (9oz) digestive biscuits
90g (3oz) salted butter, melted
500g (1lb 2oz) full-fat cream cheese
180g (6¼oz) Nutella, melted in the
    microwave and cooled, plus another
    200g (7oz) for pouring over the top
80g (2¾oz/⅔ cup) icing (powdered) sugar
4–6 Kinder Bueno chocolate bars, crushed

EQUIPMENT
20cm (8in) square cake tin—parchment
rolling pin or food processor/blender
2 mixing bowls—whisk

LINE THE TIN AND MAKE THE BASE
Line the base and sides of the tin with parchment. Blitz the biscuits in a blender or food processor to a fine crumb or just pop them in a food bag and bash them with a rolling pin (a great way to release stress!). Tip the crumbs into a bowl and mix in the melted butter, then put the mix into the base of the lined tin, pushing it down hard so it sets as one piece rather than remains crumbly. Chill in the fridge while you make the filling.

MAKE THE FILLING
Put the cream cheese in a mixing bowl with the 180g (6¼oz) cooled melted Nutella and the icing sugar and whisk until fully combined. Spread the filling over the biscuit base until flat – you might want to give it a few bangs on the work surface to help level it out.

FINISHING TOUCHES
Pour the extra melted Nutella on top, sprinkle over the crushed Kinder Bueno bars and chill in the fridge for at least 4 hours (or ideally overnight). Slice and enjoy – it's so good!

The cheesecake will store well in the fridge for up to 3 days.

ALTERNATIVE INGREDIENTS
Digestive biscuits: use any of your favourite biscuits here. Hobnobs and Oreos are two of my favourite alternatives
Nutella: use your favourite spread –a white chocolate hazelnut spread works brilliantly

Strawberries &
Cream Puff Pastries

MAKES 6 PASTRIES

British summertime isn't complete without the quintessential strawberries and cream, and these little puff pastry desserts are perfect for summer wherever you are. The light flaky pastry works so well with a jammy middle and an airy cream topped with fresh strawberries! They look like so much time and effort has gone into them.

If you're going to make them in advance make them an hour or two ahead – if they're made and left overnight the pastry will go slightly soggy.

1 x 320g (11¼oz) sheet of all-butter puff pastry

1 egg, beaten, for egg wash

200ml (7fl oz/generous ¾ cup) double (heavy) cream

1 tbsp icing (powdered) sugar

2 tsp vanilla extract

6 tsp strawberry jam

6 fresh strawberries, halved

6 little sprigs of mint

EQUIPMENT
baking tray—greaseproof paper (optional)—knife—pastry brush—mixing bowl—electric whisk—piping (icing) bag (optional)

PREHEAT THE OVEN AND LINE A BAKING TRAY
Preheat the oven to 180°C (160°C fan/350°F/gas mark 4). Line the baking tray with greaseproof paper (I use the paper that comes with the puff pastry) or use a non-stick baking tray.

BAKE THE PASTRY
Cut the pastry sheet into 6 squares, score a border 2cm (¾in) from the edge of each piece, being careful not to cut through the pastry completely (this is so we can push down the middle of each square gently after baking, to make space for the filling). Brush the pastry edges of each square with the egg wash (to give it a beautiful golden colour) and bake in the oven for 8–10 minutes, until puffed up and golden.

WHISK THE CREAM
While the pastry is in the oven, whisk the cream in a bowl to stiff peaks, then throw in the icing sugar and vanilla and whisk once more.

ASSEMBLE THE PASTRIES AND SERVE
When the pastry comes out the oven, press the middle of each square gently with your fingers so they implode gently but the borders remain puffed up. Add a teaspoon dollop of jam to the middle of each mini crater then top with the cream (you can just dollop it on, but I think it looks really pretty piped on top of the jam in zigzag formation). Decorate each pastry with a halved strawberry and a little sprig of mint. Serve!

ALTERNATIVE INGREDIENTS
Strawberries, strawberry jam: use another fresh fruit that has a jam equivalent, such as blackcurrant, raspberry or apricot.

Baileys Chocolate Mousse

This recipe is a winter staple. In the run-up to Christmas, the grown-ups in my family start popping a shot of Baileys in their hot chocolates every evening, so I wanted to make a Christmas pudding without the Christmas pudding because – quite frankly – I am just not a fan. I am, however, a huge fan of chocolate mousse and this one in particular with its boozy boost. It's great for making ahead of time.

You can make the moussse up to 3 days ahead of serving and store them in the fridge. Make and top with the cream just before serving.

FOR THE MOUSSE
100g (3½oz) milk chocolate, broken into pieces
50g (1¾oz) dark chocolate, broken into pieces
5 eggs
110ml (3¾fl oz/½ cup) Baileys
chocolate shavings of your choice, to decorate (optional)

FOR THE BAILEYS CREAM
300ml (10fl oz/1¼ cups) double (heavy) cream
1 tbsp icing (powdered) sugar
1 tbsp Baileys

EQUIPMENT
chopping board—knife—4 bowls
electric whisk—metal spoon (serving spoon or tablespoon)—4 small ramekins or 1 large serving dish

LET'S GET CHOCOLATEY
Melt the two types of chocolate in a heatproof bowl placed over a bowl of simmering water, making sure the bowl doesn't touch the water (or, alternatively, melt it in the microwave). Set aside to cool slightly while you separate the eggs, putting the yolks and whites in separate, clean bowls. Stir the egg yolks into the slightly cooled chocolate to form a chocolatey paste, then pour in the Baileys and mix really well (it will form a smooth chocolate mixture after a minute or two of mixing). Set aside.

WHISK THE EGG WHITES
Whisk the egg whites in the other bowl until they form stiff peaks (when you take the whisk out, the peaks of whisked white should stand firm). Add half the egg whites to the chocolate mixture and fold them in with the metal spoon in a figure-of-8 movement until there are no white bits showing (this way you don't knock the air out of the egg whites and the mix stays light and moussy). Fold in the remaining egg whites.

CHILL
Gently spoon the chocolate mousse into the ramekins or serving dish and chill in the fridge for 3–4 hours.

FINISHING TOUCHES
Using an electric whisk, whisk the double cream until thick, then add the icing sugar and Baileys and whisk again to combine. Either spoon the cream on top of the mousse and spread it out or, for a special occasion, pipe a little swirl on top then grate over a little more chocolate (at Christmas I add a little pinch of edible gold dust) – it's the perfect celebration pudding!

ALTERNATIVE INGREDIENTS
Baileys: use a creamed rum or other creamy liquor (mint chocolate Baileys gives a mint chocolate hint to the mousse)
Chocolate: use 100g (3½oz) dark chocolate and 50g (1¾oz) milk chocolate

Peanut Butter &
Jam Sponge Cake

This cake combines a childlike sandwich filling with everyone's favourite sweet treat... cake! A quick-to-whip-up cake that will please everyone from 5-year-olds to 85-year-olds, the three tiers makes it look really dramatic (with no extra effort). You don't have to use any fancy equipment – the homemade look adds charm!

350g (12½oz) salted butter, softened, plus extra for greasing
350g (12½oz/1½ cups) caster (superfine) sugar
5 medium eggs
2 tsp vanilla extract
350g (12½oz/2½ cups) self-raising flour

FOR THE BUTTERCREAM
250g (9oz) salted butter, softened
3 tbsp smooth peanut butter
250g (9oz/2 cups) icing (powdered) sugar

TO FILL AND DECORATE
3 tsp smooth peanut butter
3 tbsp strawberry jam
a handful of chopped peanuts

EQUIPMENT
3 x 20cm (8in) round cake tins—2 mixing bowls—electric whisk—toothpick or skewer

PREHEAT THE OVEN AND PREPARE THE TINS
Preheat the oven to 180°C (160°C fan/350°F/gas mark 4) and grease all three cake tins.

MAKE THE CAKES
Cream the butter and sugar in a mixing bowl with an electric whisk or wooden spoon until light and fluffy. Add the eggs, one at a time, beating well after each addition, then stir in the vanilla extract and fold in the flour. Divide evenly among the three prepared tins and bang the tins on the surface a couple of times to release any air bubbles. Bake for 20–25 minutes, until golden brown and when you press the top they spring back and a skewer comes out clean.

MAKE THE BUTTERCREAM
While the cakes are in the oven, make the buttercream. Using an electric whisk, whisk the butter in a bowl for 8 minutes until really pale and fluffy, then spoon in the peanut butter and whisk for another minute before adding the icing sugar, a third at a time.

COOL THEN ICE THE SPONGES
Remove the cakes from the oven and leave to cool for 10 minutes before removing from the tins to a wire rack. Leave to cool completely. If your cooled sponges are domed and you want to level them out, just carefully cut off the tops. Spread some buttercream over the top of one sponge, then add some strawberry jam and a dollop of peanut butter in the middle. Top with the second sponge and repeat. Top with the third sponge and add a final layer of buttercream. In straight(ish) lines, add the jam and peanut butter, then drag a toothpick or a skewer through in opposing lines on top – this makes it look like organised mess! Finally, scatter over the chopped peanuts.

SERVE
Slice up, serve and enjoy (I really recommend having a slice with a cup of tea to wash it down!). The cake will keep in a cake tin or sealed container for about 3 days at room temperature, or up to 5 days in a container in the fridge.

Simply Delicious Brownies

A brownie is such a perfect Sunday treat, scattered with your choice of nuts and chocolate. These are the gooiest, richest, most irresistible brownies you'll make, and they are so delicious. The crunch from the nuts and the soft melted chocolate just works. If you're a big kid and don't like your brownies messed with, just swap the nuts for more chocolate chips (but keep the ground almonds: you can't taste it but that's what makes them gooey brownies).

70g (2½oz) salted butter
250g (9oz/generous cup) caster (superfine) sugar
2 medium eggs plus 1 egg yolk
2 tsp vanilla extract
80ml (2¾fl oz/ ⅓ cup) sunflower or vegetable oil
75g (2½oz) cocoa powder
½ tsp baking powder
65g (2 ⅓oz/generous ⅓ cup) ground almonds (almond meal)
1 tbsp plain (all-purpose) flour
40g (1½oz) pecans, chopped
40g (1½oz) slivered almonds
40g (1½oz) chocolate chips of your choice

EQUIPMENT
20cm (8in) square cake tin—parchment
saucepan—wooden spoon or spatula
small bowl—skewer

PREHEAT THE OVEN AND LINE TIN
Preheat the oven to 180°C (160°C fan/350°F/gas mark 4) and line the tin with parchment.

MAKE THE BROWNIE BATTER
Melt the butter with the sugar in the saucepan over a low heat. When the sugar has dissolved, remove from the heat and allow it to cool slightly (so the eggs don't scramble). Add the eggs and egg yolk along with the vanilla extract and oil. In a small bowl, stir together the cocoa powder, baking powder, ground almonds and flour until well combined. Pour into the egg mixture and stir well until you have a lump-free batter. Throw in the nuts and chocolate chips then spread the batter out in the lined tin so it's level.

BAKE!
Bake the brownie in the oven for 25–30 minutes, until the top is cooked and shiny and a skewer comes out sticky but not coated in raw mixture.

COOL, SLICE AND SERVE
Remove from the oven – it's going to be super gooey in the middle which means it will be HOT, so allow it to cool in the tin for 15–20 minutes – it will still be warm, but will be more manageable to slice. Slice into slabs of yumminess and serve.

The brownies will keep in a sealed container for about 3 days at room temperature, or up to 5 days in a container in the fridge.

ALTERNATIVE INGREDIENTS
Butter: use margarine or baking spread
Neutral oil: use melted butter, margarine or cooking/baking spread
Nuts and chocolate chips: use your favourite nuts or brownie fillings – hazelnuts and pretzels work well

Drink Pairings

When I serve my comfort food, I like to accompany it with a delicious drink. Here are my recommended pairings for the recipes in this book.

SALADS AND LIGHTER DISHES
To accompany light dishes with fruity or tart flavours, such as the Raspberry, Nectarine and Mozzarella Salad (see page 14), you want something light that complements the dish and doesn't overpower the delicate flavours.

BEERS
A light crisp lager works well, such as a Corona, Coors or Heineken.

WINES
Opt for something crisp and refreshing such as a pinot grigio, riesling, Chablis, chardonnay, chenin blanc, Provençal rosé, Champagne, cava or prosecco.

SOFT DRINKS
Sparkling flavoured water, elderflower drinks and bitter lemonades.

OILY DISHES
To accompany any of the filling dishes in this book, including fried dishes or some of the fish dishes that are oily such as the Beer-battered Fish Sandwich (see page 154), you want something that will cut through the oils and cleanse your palette.

BEERS AND ALES
Go for a lighter lager or IPA/pale ale.

WHITE WINES
Go for something light. Fizzy wines work well – prosecco, cava, Champagne, riesling, sauvignon blanc, chardonnay, chenin blanc or pinot grigio.

SOFT DRINKS
A tart lemonade that has a bitterness to it, or a sparkling flavoured water.

RICH AND MEATY DISHES
You're going to want something full-bodied to complement the richness and break through the meaty flavours of dishes such as Skiing Steak Frites (see page 114).

BEERS AND ALES
Go for a hoppy beer and something with bubbles. IPAs and pale ales work here.

WINES
Go for something bold and full-bodied for fatty, richer meats, or a lighter medium-bodied wine for leaner meats. Syrah or shiraz, cabernet sauvignon, malbec, merlot, tempranillo, Bordeaux, Châteauneuf-du-Pape all work well.

SOFT DRINKS
Something sweet such as a coca cola works nicely, but also a simple soda with lime juice is really good at cutting through the bold flavours.

CHICKEN DISHES
Chicken dishes need fresh flavoured wines that complement the food while not overpowering and masking the flavours in the dish.

WINES

For chicken salads (see page 81), go for lighter wines, such as rosés. For chicken pies, opt for something a little richer. Dishes such as Pulled Chicken Tacos (see page 132) or fried chicken (see page 143) can actually be better suited to a fizzy wine like a Champagne or prosecco. For chicken risottos (see page 87) and my roast dinners (see pages 157 and 167), I love red wine.

Rich white wines: chardonnay, chenin blanc, riesling, muscat, sauvignon blanc.

Lighter white wines: riesling, pinot grigio, sauvignon blanc.

Rosé: Provençal rosé, pinot noir rosé, white zinfandel.

SOFT DRINKS

Full-flavoured drinks that are sweet and fruity: a juice is always a good option.

CREAMY DISHES

You want something bold, maybe slightly oaky, with a little acidity to cut through the richness of the cream and work as a palette cleanser while complementing dishes such as Creamy Tuna Pasta (see page 32) and Hug-in-a-bowl Beef Stroganoff (see page 60).

BEERS

Classic lagers, like Peroni, Moretti, Stella Artois and San Miguel, work nicely but you can also play around with IPAs, pale ales and fruity beers.

WINES

White wines: sauvignon blanc, oaked Italian trebbiano, white rioja, chardonnay.

Red wines: cabernet sauvignon, pinot noir, merlot.

SOFT DRINKS

Something light and sweet like a sparkling elderflower and soda.

SPICY FOODS

Dishes such as Harisssa Chickpea and Halloumi Salad (see page 26) and Dad's Proper Chilli (see page 165) want something that is going to enhance the flavour of the food, especially if you've gone to all the work to add all those flavours in there.

BEERS

A wheaty or hoppy beer is lovely here, such as Blue Moon (with a slice of orange), Hoegaarden, Hefeweizen or Hop House.

WINES

Try a spicy red wine or a wine with sweetness to complement any chilli heat, or something light and slightly earthy such as a pinot noir, tempranillo, merlot, syrah, malbec, riesling or grenache.

SOFT DRINKS

Opt for a palette cleanser, like a citrussy or fruity sparkling drink.

Index

Acknowledgements

Writing this book was harder than I thought it would be, but also more rewarding than I could have ever dreamed. I wouldn't have been able to do it without the amazing people mentioned below. I have met people throughout this journey that I now class as very dear friends and will be working with for the rest of my life because of their hard work, kindness and immense support in helping me create *Country Comfort*.

Firstly, I want to thank my incredible family: my momma, sister, grandparents and dad. Your continued support and endless words of encouragement over the years gave me the courage to put pen to paper. Words can't describe how grateful and lucky I am to have such a supportive family. Thank you for helping me with the animals when I was writing late at night, for your generosity as I invaded our kitchen to crack down on the recipes, and for your love and hugs when things may not have been going perfectly. You all had things going on in your life that were equally as important as this book, and you put them to one side to help me make my dream a reality.

My incredible publishing team at Quarto, and the photographers and food stylists: Eleanor Maxfield, Charlotte Frost, Claire Rochford, Saskia Sidey and Daniel Jones. You got on board with my vision immediately and went above and beyond to make this book reality and help me achieve my dream of becoming an author. I will be forever grateful to you, wonderful people. This book wouldn't be here without you and that's something I will never forget.

My management and literary agent, Oscar Janson-Smith, Emily Louise Gray and Rosie Luff, for helping me find my Quarto family, supporting me with each meeting and crying happy tears with me each step of the way.

My partner, for eating so many trial recipes, for the endless words of encouragement and love, and never having any words other than 'you've got this', even if I didn't think I could do it myself. And my friends, for helping me believe in my career, for the uplifting phone calls and messages over the years, and making me who I am today. I am lucky to have each and every one of you.

Finally, thanks to my followers. Whether you've been here since my first post, or you're new to my recipes, or you've just picked up this book and are now making comfort food with your loved ones, without you making my recipes over the years, commenting and messaging me with words of kindness, and asking for this book, it wouldn't have been made! I am forever grateful – this book is for you. Thank you.

About the author

Hari Beavis, the creative force behind 'Baking with Beavis' and 'Peeled Back', has skyrocketed to social media stardom in the foodie realm. Boasting over 700K followers, Hari's delicious content features classic comfort foods and decadent treats, captivating audiences with each mouth-watering creation. With her mission to make home cooking more accessible for a wider audience, Hari infuses her recipes with simplicity and flair, inspiring both novice and seasoned cooks alike. Her impressive engagement and dynamic online presence have secured partnerships with prestigious brands like Tesco, Morphy Richards, Coca-Cola, and L'Oreal, cementing her status as a leading influencer in the culinary sphere.

Quarto

First published in 2024 by Carnival
an imprint of The Quarto Group.
One Triptych Place, London, SE1 9SH
United Kingdom
T (0)20 7700 6700
www.Quarto.com

A catalogue record for this book is available from the British
Library.

ISBN 978-0-7112-9789-0
EBOOK ISBN 978-0-7112-9790-6

10 9 8 7 6 5 4 3 2 1

Book Designer: Claire Rochford
Editors: Charlotte Frost and Katerina Menhennet
Food Stylist: Saskia Sidey
Food Styling Assistant: Imogen Mucklow
Illustrator: Ryn Frank Ltd
Photographer: Dan Jones
Photography Assistant: Rosie Alsop
Prop Stylist: Max Robinson
Publisher: Eleanor Maxfield
Senior Designer: Isabel Eeles
Senior Production Manager: Eliza Walsh

Printed in China